LUTON LIBRARIES

BOOKS SHOULD BE RETURNED BY THE LAST DATE STAMPED

For Renewals
01582 547413
www.lutonlibrary.com

D1343635

ALLEN GINSBERG

Poems selected by MARK FORD

faber and faber

First published in 2008
by Faber and Faber Limited
Bloomsbury House, 74-77 Great Russell Street, London WC1B 3DA

Photoset by RefineCatch Ltd, Bungay, Suffolk
Printed in England by CPI Group (UK) Ltd, Croydon, CR0 4YY

A CIP record for this book
is available from the British Library

ISBN 978-0-571-23810-1

Contents

Introduction

For much of his writing life Allen Ginsberg was the most famous poet on the planet. His readings in America and around the world attracted rock-concert-sized audiences, and posters of him, straggle-bearded, and only half ironically sporting an Uncle Sam hat atop his luxuriant, unruly hair, adorned the walls of innumerable campus dorms and hippie communes. 'He unlocks our chains,' Emerson wrote of the true poet, 'and admits us to a new scene.' The scene to which Ginsberg admitted his myriad contemporary readers was one of free love, LSD, political activism, shared living arrangements, beads, incense, mantras, and Eastern-influenced questing after enlightenment.

The counterculture, of which Ginsberg was the poetic figurehead, achieved its fullest eZorescence in the late sixties, the era of be-ins and flower power and Haight-Ashbury, but its literary origins can be traced back to the winter of 1943–44 when Ginsberg, then in his freshman year at Columbia, was introduced to two ambitious but unpublished would-be writers, William Burroughs and Jack Kerouac. Already somewhat disillusioned with the staid approach to literary studies promulgated by such as Lionel Trilling at Columbia, Ginsberg found in the sweeping, anarchic wit of Burroughs and the reckless, infectious energy of Kerouac just the catalysts he needed to initiate the release of his own rebellious instincts. Within a year or two he'd begun what would become a lifelong interest in illegal drugs, been suspended from Columbia for writing obscenities in the grime on his dormitory window, and had his first homosexual encounter – with a hustler he picked up in the Hotel Astor Bar in Times Square.

The heroic deeds of the assorted mavericks with whom Ginsberg hung out during his chequered career at Columbia are mythically celebrated in the opening section of his most famous poem, 'Howl', begun in the summer of 1955 and given its legendary first reading at the Six Gallery in San Francisco on 7 October of that year. On the bill with Ginsberg were Philip Lamantia, Michael McClure, Philip Whalen and Gary Snyder. Kenneth Rexroth, the prime mover behind the San Francisco Renaissance, introduced, but it was Jack Kerouac who did most to ensure the evening's success by circulating several gallon-jugs of red wine. When a somewhat tipsy Ginsberg – giving what was only his second ever public reading – took to the stage, Kerouac urged him on with shouts of 'Go, man!' and 'Yeah!', and then kept time to the poem's vatic strophes by tapping on an empty wine jug. The next morning the elated poet received a telegram from Lawrence Ferlinghetti of City Lights press modelled on Emerson's letter to Whitman on receiving the first edition of *Leaves of Grass* – published, incidentally, exactly a hundred years earlier: 'I greet you at the beginning of a great career – When do I get manuscript of *Howl*?'

Howl and Other Poems duly appeared a year later, only to be impounded by the customs authorities, and ludicrously arraigned and put on trial for obscenity. 'I saw the best minds of my generation destroyed by madness,' the poem opens, then proceeds by chronicling the deranged exploits, impassioned yearnings and sexual triumphs of a holy band of desperadoes, a set of 'angelheaded hipsters burning for the ancient heavenly connection to the starry dynamo in the machinery of night'. The poem elides their names and makes them into a kind of tribal collective, all for one and one for all:

> who howled on their knees in the subway and were dragged
> 　　off the roof waving genitals and manuscripts,
> who let themselves be fucked in the ass by saintly
> 　　motorcyclists, and screamed with joy,
> who blew and were blown by those human seraphim, the
> 　　sailors, caresses of Atlantic and Caribbean love,
> who balled in the morning in the evenings in rosegardens
> 　　and the grass of public parks and cemeteries scattering
> 　　their semen freely to whomever come who may

Whitman had famously imagined himself 'jetting the stuff of far more arrogant republics', and dissemination of the Beat word was often figured by Ginsberg, too, as a joyous, indiscriminate scattering of body-seed by himself and his (all-male) fellow initiates.

The trial was intended to purge straight-laced, God-fearing mid-fifties America of such images of deviance and pollution. It turned out, inevitably, to be the springboard for Ginsberg's immense and enduring fame. It was covered widely in the media, and launched the concept of the Beatnik (a term coined by analogy to that other challenge to American national pride, sputnik). The prosecution mustered only two somewhat dubious witnesses: David Kirk, an assistant professor of English at the University of San Francisco, declared 'Howl' of 'negligible' literary value because too closely imitative of Whitman – but such an assessment hardly justified banning the poem; and one Gail Potter, after distributing little brochures announcing the lessons she offered in speech and diction, and revealing, to the overflowing gallery's great amusement, that she had rewritten both *Faust* and *Everyman*, complained that 'you feel like you are going through the gutter when you have to read that stuff. I didn't linger on it too long, I assure you.' In his final ruling Judge Clayton Horn insisted that to impose 'vapid, innocuous euphemism' on Ginsberg's graphic and figurative language would be to violate the First and Fourteenth Amendments.

Ginsberg once declared 'Howl', some of which he wrote after taking a dose of peyote, to be his 'breakthru' poem, and certainly its wildly uninhibited diction and its straightforward political message ('Moloch whose blood is running money! Moloch whose fingers are ten armies!') appealed to a great swathe of readers uninterested in the dry ironies and formal intricacies of the standard mid-century Anglo-American lyric. Ginsberg's principal touchstones were Blake – who once appeared to him in a room in a brownstone in Harlem and recited 'Ah! Sun-Flower' and 'The Sick Rose' in a deep, unearthly voice – and Whitman, whom he imagines meeting, in one of the best of his shorter poems, in a supermarket in California:

I saw you, Walt Whitman, childless, lonely old grubber,
>poking among the meats in the refrigerator and eyeing
>the grocery boys.
I heard you asking questions of each: Who killed the pork
>chops? What price bananas? Are you my Angel?
I wandered in and out of the brilliant stacks of cans
>following you, and followed in my imagination by the
>store detective.
We strode down the open corridors together in our solitary
>fancy, tasting artichokes, possessing every frozen
>delicacy, and never passing the cashier.

Where are we going, Walt Whitman? The doors close in an
>hour. Which way does your beard point tonight?

Eager to follow in their prophetic footsteps, Ginsberg saw himself as a national bard whose mission was to rescue his country from itself: from its corrupt politicians, from its military-industrial complex, from the machinations of its secret services (who kept voluminous files on him), from the iniquities and deceits of capitalism, and from the 'mustard gas of sinister intelligent editors' who determined both the news agenda and the culture that blinded his fellow citizens to the truth. A poem such as 'Howl', although in many ways radically new, can also be seen as a mid-twentieth-century version of that most venerable of American genres, the Jeremiad, which warns the writer's countrymen of impending disaster if they keep ignoring their spiritual health. Like, say, Michael Wigglesworth's *The Day of Doom*, a best-seller in New England in the late seventeenth century, or Thoreau's *Walden*, 'Howl' abjures its readers to cast off their false selves, to reject Moloch's 'demonic industries!' so as to recover a lost vision of the ideal or sacred. Once liberated from what Blake called our 'mind-forged manacles', it will become instantly clear that all is redeemed and to be celebrated: 'The world is holy! The soul is holy! The skin is holy! The nose is holy! The tongue and cock and hand and asshole holy!' Even, or so the 'Footnote to Howl' tells us, 'Holy the cocks of the grandfathers of Kansas!'

Ginsberg discovered his distinctive idiom, with its instantly recognisable mix of the rhapsodic and the picaresque, the candid and the outrageous, after years of uncertain poetic prospecting. His early work ranges from pastiche Elizabethan love lyrics to flat, Williams-inspired descriptions of New Jersey cityscapes. It was only in the poems composed after his move to the West Coast in 1954 that Ginsberg really began to put into practice Kerouac's ideals of spontaneous composition, of 'unrepressed wordslinging': 'that was the first time I sat down to blow,' he enthused in a letter to Kerouac describing the genesis of 'Howl'. In emulation of their bebop heroes, pre-eminent among whom was Charlie Parker, Kerouac and Ginsberg sought to make the act of writing into the equivalent of an improvised riff; *On the Road* was famously written on a vast scroll of typewriter paper in three frenetic weeks in April of 1951, and Ginsberg's 'Howl' and 'Kaddish' were similarly the result of intense, extended sessions of compositional fervour. Crucial also to Ginsberg's sudden coming into his own in the poems collected in *Howl* was his abandoning of his long-drawn out fight against his homosexuality. Like many queer men of his generation, Ginsberg had invested much time and money in search of a psychoanalytical cure for his condition. In San Francisco he started seeing a Dr Hicks, who, to his great surprise, seemed unfazed by the fact he loved men. He encouraged Ginsberg to give up his job in marketing, not to feel guilty about his passion for his latest flame, Peter Orlovsky, who was destined to become his lifelong partner, and to write poems. This timely advice had a powerful effect. 'America,' Ginsberg declared defiantly in the poem of that name, written in January of 1956, 'I'm putting my queer shoulder to the wheel.'

This involved not only attempting to save America by embodying his Beat visions and experiences in a new, more open kind of poetry, but forging a sense of communal purpose among such disparate Beat talents as the gun-toting Burroughs, the anarchy-loving Gregory Corso, the Zen Buddhist Gary Snyder and the libertarian Kerouac, who in his later years became a staunch supporter of the extreme right-wing presidential candidate Barry Goldwater. Indeed, aside from their friendship with Ginsberg – and indebtedness to him for promoting their careers – these writers shared little beyond an extreme, but not particularly unusual, disaffection with the conformities of Eisenhower's America. The public's ready response to their howls of protest rather belies Robert Lowell's vision at the end of the fifties of a decade happily 'tranquillized'. Ginsberg was by far the most media-savvy of the group, and the only one really invested in presenting them to the public at large – and to literary historians of the future – as a coherent movement. As early as 1952 he enthused to Kerouac that 'already we have the nucleus of a totally new historically important American creation.' Kerouac begged to differ, pointing out they just happened to be writers who were friends.

Kerouac eventually found the fame his work brought him almost intolerable, but Ginsberg thrived both on his celebrity and the multiple controversies it aroused. He particularly loved baiting the Academy: 'the trouble with these creeps,' he observed in 1960 of all those embowered in university literature departments, 'is they wouldn't know Poetry if it came up and buggered them in broad daylight.' He also developed into an eloquent spokesperson for a wide range of political causes, and through his not-for-profit organisation, the Committee on Poetry, did battle with the authorities on any number of fronts. He campaigned against censorship, against United Fruit's exploitation of Central America, against nuclear bombs, for the legalisation of drugs, for the lowering of the age of consent – even contributing funds to NAMBLA (the North American Man Boy Love Association). Much of his poetry is explicitly political, and it's worth pointing out that poetry and politics dominated his formative years in Paterson, New Jersey – the town immortalised by William Carlos Williams in his epic *Paterson*, published in five books between 1946 and 1958. His mother, Naomi, was active in Communist circles until she suffered a series of devastating breakdowns, while his father (a high-school teacher of English literature by profession), was a lyric poet in his spare time, though one who had to subsidise publication of his work – it cost poor Louis $2,000 to persuade the firm of Liveright to issue his second volume, *The Everlasting Minute*. His impersonal, delicate lyrics could hardly be further from his son's impassioned confessions and injunctions, and they must have made an interesting double-act when performing together, as they did on a number of occasions in the late sixties.

Needless to say, not all of Ginsberg's directly political poetry transcends its topical origins. It was the Vietnam War that most fully united the disparate forces of American dissent, and in the long poems collected in *The Fall of America: Poems of These States* (1972), he attempted an ambitious, almost epic catalogue of mid-Sixties America, positing his own countercultural values and perspectives against the establishment rhetoric saturating the airwaves and news columns. Ginsberg used a tape-recorder to preserve his impressions and observations while he and his entourage zigzagged in a VW bus from reading to reading across the country. I include here 'Wichita Vortex Sutra' (composed in February of 1966), which splices together radio bulletins, snatches of pop songs ('Angelic Dylan singing across the nation / "When all your children start to resent you / Won't you come see me, Queen Jane?" '), newspaper headlines ('Omaha World Herald – *Rusk Says Toughness / Essential for Peace*'), and a dizzying series of 'democratic vistas' and pastoral snapshots; the result is a loose, rambling, alternative state-of-the-nation address. The form and methods of Ginsberg's *Fall of America* poems owe much to Ezra Pound's *Cantos*, although the two poets' political convictions were of course wholly antithetical. The volume's fire is trained in particular on the manipulation of language by politicians and the media:

> The war is language
>   language abused
>   for Advertisement
>   language used
> like magic for power on the planet

Black magic language,
  formulas for reality –
    Communism is a 9 letter word
      used by inferior magicians with
the wrong alchemical formula for transforming earth into
  gold

In their wide-angled way, these poems capture the spirit of the times with a fullness and freshness that elevate them above the great mass of political poetry generated by the war. Yet fearing that those in power might not heed his message when delivered poetically, Ginsberg also sent off numerous long letters to politicians urging them to mend their ways; in 1966, for instance, he wrote to Robert McNamara, then Secretary of Defence, rebuking him for sending out 'waves of anxiety and fear', and advising him to search for inner peace by reading Buddhist texts and listening to Bob Dylan.

It is surely, though, as an elegist that Ginsberg is at his most expressive and moving. His uncensoring eye for detail renders his posthumous portraits of such as Aunt Rose, Neal Cassady and his parents at once vivid, memorable, and tender.

Aunt Rose – now – might I see you
with your thin face and buck tooth smile and pain
    of rheumatism – and a long black heavy shoe
     for your bony left leg
limping down the long hall in Newark on the running carpet
    past the black grand piano
      in the day room
        where the parties were
   and I sang Spanish loyalist songs
      in a high squeaky voice
        (hysterical) the committee listening
      while you limped around the room
       collected the money –

Ginsberg himself had to sign the papers authorising Naomi's lobotomy in 1947, when he was only twenty, and in 'Kaddish' (1957–9) he recalled the nature and effects of her worsening paranoia with unsparing precision. Twenty-five years on she returned to haunt him in one of the most effective of his later poems, 'White Shroud', this time accosting him in the guise of a bag lady holed up in an alleyway in the Bronx. And she makes a final, fleeting appearance in a very late poem that is almost a self-elegy; in 'Objective Subject', composed a matter of weeks before his own death in April of 1997, Ginsberg allows himself to ponder the particular nature of the poetic and physical bodies he is about to leave behind:

It's true I write about myself
Who else do I know so well?
Where else gather blood red roses & kitchen garbage
What else has my thick heart, hepatitis, or hemorrhoids –
Who else lived my seventy years, my old Naomi?
and if by chance I scribe U.S. politics, Wisdom
meditation, theories of art
it's because I read a newspaper loved
teachers skimmed books or visited a museum.

MARK FORD

ALLEN GINSBERG

Dream Record: June 8, 1955

A drunken night in my house with a
boy, San Francisco: I lay asleep:
darkness:
        I went back to Mexico City
and saw Joan Burroughs leaning
forward in a garden chair, arms
on her knees. She studied me with
clear eyes and downcast smile, her
face restored to a fine beauty
tequila and salt had made strange
before the bullet in her brow.

We talked of the life since then.
Well, what's Burroughs doing now?
Bill on earth, he's in North Africa.
Oh, and Kerouac? Jack still jumps
with the same beat genius as before,
notebooks filled with Buddha.
I hope he makes it, she laughed.
Is Huncke still in the can? No,
last time I saw him on Times Square.
And how is Kenney? Married, drunk
and golden in the East. You? New
loves in the West –
        Then I knew
she was a dream: and questioned her
– Joan, what kind of knowledge have
the dead? can you still love
your mortal acquaintances?
What do you remember of us?
        She
faded in front of me – The next instant
I saw her rain-stained tombstone

rear an illegible epitaph
under the gnarled branch of a small
tree in the wild grass
of an unvisited garden in Mexico.

Howl

For Carl Solomon

I

I saw the best minds of my generation destroyed by madness,
    starving hysterical naked,

dragging themselves through the negro streets at dawn looking
    for an angry fix,

angelheaded hipsters burning for the ancient heavenly connec-
    tion to the starry dynamo in the machinery of night,

who poverty and tatters and hollow-eyed and high sat up
    smoking in the supernatural darkness of cold-water flats
    floating across the tops of cities contemplating jazz,

who bared their brains to Heaven under the El and saw
    Mohammedan angels staggering on tenement roofs
    illuminated,

who passed through universities with radiant cool eyes halluci-
    nating Arkansas and Blake-light tragedy among the
    scholars of war,

who were expelled from the academies for crazy & publishing
    obscene odes on the windows of the skull,

who cowered in unshaven rooms in underwear, burning their
    money in wastebaskets and listening to the Terror through
    the wall,

who got busted in their pubic beards returning through Laredo
    with a belt of marijuana for New York,

who ate fire in paint hotels or drank turpentine in Paradise
    Alley, death, or purgatoried their torsos night after
    night

with dreams, with drugs, with waking nightmares, alcohol and
    cock and endless balls,

incomparable blind streets of shuddering cloud and lightning
    in the mind leaping toward poles of Canada & Paterson,
    illuminating all the motionless world of Time between,

Peyote solidities of halls, backyard green tree cemetery dawns, wine drunkenness over the rooftops, storefront boroughs of teahead joyride neon blinking traffic light, sun and moon and tree vibrations in the roaring winter dusks of Brooklyn, ashcan rantings and kind king light of mind,

who chained themselves to subways for the endless ride from Battery to holy Bronx on benzedrine until the noise of wheels and children brought them down shuddering mouth-wracked and battered bleak of brain all drained of brilliance in the drear light of Zoo,

who sank all night in submarine light of Bickford's floated out and sat through the stale beer afternoon in desolate Fugazzi's, listening to the crack of doom on the hydrogen jukebox,

who talked continuously seventy hours from park to pad to bar to Bellevue to museum to the Brooklyn Bridge,

a lost battalion of platonic conversationalists jumping down the stoops off fire escapes off windowsills off Empire State out of the moon,

yacketayakking screaming vomiting whispering facts and memories and anecdotes and eyeball kicks and shocks of hospitals and jails and wars,

whole intellects disgorged in total recall for seven days and nights with brilliant eyes, meat for the Synagogue cast on the pavement,

who vanished into nowhere Zen New Jersey leaving a trail of ambiguous picture postcards of Atlantic City Hall,

suffering Eastern sweats and Tangerian bone-grindings and migraines of China under junk-withdrawal in Newark's bleak furnished room,

who wandered around and around at midnight in the railroad yard wondering where to go, and went, leaving no broken hearts,

who lit cigarettes in boxcars boxcars boxcars racketing through snow toward lonesome farms in grandfather night,

who studied Plotinus Poe St. John of the Cross telepathy and
bop kabbalah because the cosmos instinctively vibrated at
their feet in Kansas,

who loned it through the streets of Idaho seeking visionary
indian angels who were visionary indian angels,

who thought they were only mad when Baltimore gleamed in
supernatural ecstasy,

who jumped in limousines with the Chinaman of Oklahoma on
the impulse of winter midnight streetlight smalltown rain,

who lounged hungry and lonesome through Houston seeking
jazz or sex or soup, and followed the brilliant Spaniard to
converse about America and Eternity, a hopeless task, and
so took ship to Africa,

who disappeared into the volcanoes of Mexico leaving behind
nothing but the shadow of dungarees and the lava and ash
of poetry scattered in fireplace Chicago,

who reappeared on the West Coast investigating the FBI in
beards and shorts with big pacifist eyes sexy in their dark
skin passing out incomprehensible leaflets,

who burned cigarette holes in their arms protesting the narcotic
tobacco haze of Capitalism,

who distributed Supercommunist pamphlets in Union Square
weeping and undressing while the sirens of Los Alamos
wailed them down, and wailed down Wall, and the Staten
Island ferry also wailed,

who broke down crying in white gymnasiums naked and trembling before the machinery of other skeletons,

who bit detectives in the neck and shrieked with delight in
policecars for committing no crime but their own wild
cooking pederasty and intoxication,

who howled on their knees in the subway and were dragged off
the roof waving genitals and manuscripts,

who let themselves be fucked in the ass by saintly motorcyclists,
and screamed with joy,

who blew and were blown by those human seraphim, the
sailors, caresses of Atlantic and Caribbean love,

who balled in the morning in the evenings in rosegardens and the grass of public parks and cemeteries scattering their semen freely to whomever come who may,

who hiccuped endlessly trying to giggle but wound up with a sob behind a partition in a Turkish Bath when the blond & naked angel came to pierce them with a sword,

who lost their loveboys to the three old shrews of fate the one eyed shrew of the heterosexual dollar the one eyed shrew that winks out of the womb and the one eyed shrew that does nothing but sit on her ass and snip the intellectual golden threads of the craftsman's loom,

who copulated ecstatic and insatiate with a bottle of beer a sweetheart a package of cigarettes a candle and fell off the bed, and continued along the floor and down the hall and ended fainting on the wall with a vision of ultimate cunt and come eluding the last gyzym of consciousness,

who sweetened the snatches of a million girls trembling in the sunset, and were red eyed in the morning but prepared to sweeten the snatch of the sunrise, flashing buttocks under barns and naked in the lake,

who went out whoring through Colorado in myriad stolen night-cars, N.C., secret hero of these poems, cocksman and Adonis of Denver – joy to the memory of his innumerable lays of girls in empty lots & diner backyards, moviehouses' rickety rows, on mountaintops in caves or with gaunt waitresses in familiar roadside lonely petticoat upliftings & especially secret gas-station solipsisms of johns, & hometown alleys too,

who faded out in vast sordid movies, were shifted in dreams, woke on a sudden Manhattan, and picked themselves up out of basements hungover with heartless Tokay and horrors of Third Avenue iron dreams & stumbled to unemployment offices,

who walked all night with their shoes full of blood on the snow-bank docks waiting for a door in the East River to open to a room full of steam-heat and opium, who created great suicidal dramas on the apartment cliff-banks of the Hudson under the wartime blue floodlight of the moon & their heads shall be crowned with laurel in oblivion,

who ate the lamb stew of the imagination or digested the crab at the muddy bottom of the rivers of Bowery,

who wept at the romance of the streets with their pushcarts full of onions and bad music,

who sat in boxes breathing in the darkness under the bridge, and rose up to build harpsichords in their lofts,

who coughed on the sixth floor of Harlem crowned with flame under the tubercular sky surrounded by orange crates of theology,

who scribbled all night rocking and rolling over lofty incantations which in the yellow morning were stanzas of gibberish,

who cooked rotten animals lung heart feet tail borsht & tortillas dreaming of the pure vegetable kingdom,

who plunged themselves under meat trucks looking for an egg,

who threw their watches off the roof to cast their ballot for Eternity outside of Time, & alarm clocks fell on their heads every day for the next decade,

who cut their wrists three times successively unsuccessfully, gave up and were forced to open antique stores where they thought they were growing old and cried,

who were burned alive in their innocent flannel suits on Madison Avenue amid blasts of leaden verse & the tanked-up clatter of the iron regiments of fashion & the nitroglycerine shrieks of the fairies of advertising & the mustard gas of sinister intelligent editors, or were run down by the drunken taxicabs of Absolute Reality,

who jumped off the Brooklyn Bridge this actually happened and walked away unknown and forgotten into the ghostly daze of Chinatown soup alleyways & firetrucks, not even one free beer,

who sang out of their windows in despair, fell out of the subway window, jumped in the filthy Passaic, leaped on negroes,

cried all over the street, danced on broken wineglasses
   barefoot smashed phonograph records of nostalgic
   European 1930s German jazz finished the whiskey and
   threw up groaning into the bloody toilet, moans in their
   ears and the blast of colossal steamwhistles,
who barreled down the highways of the past journeying to each
   other's hotrod-Golgotha jail-solitude watch or Birmingham
   jazz incarnation,
who drove crosscountry seventytwo hours to find out if I had a
   vision or you had a vision or he had a vision to find out
   Eternity,
who journeyed to Denver, who died in Denver, who came back
   to Denver & waited in vain, who watched over Denver &
   brooded & loned in Denver and finally went away to find
   out the Time, & now Denver is lonesome for her heroes,
who fell on their knees in hopeless cathedrals praying for each
   other's salvation and light and breasts, until the soul
   illuminated its hair for a second,
who crashed through their minds in jail waiting for impossible
   criminals with golden heads and the charm of reality in
   their hearts who sang sweet blues to Alcatraz,
who retired to Mexico to cultivate a habit, or Rocky Mount to
   tender Buddha or Tangiers to boys or Southern Pacific to
   the black locomotive or Harvard to Narcissus to Woodlawn
   to the daisychain or grave,
who demanded sanity trials accusing the radio of hypnotism &
   were left with their insanity & their hands & a hung jury,
who threw potato salad at CCNY lecturers on Dadaism and
   subsequently presented themselves on the granite steps of
   the madhouse with shaven heads and harlequin speech of
   suicide, demanding instantaneous lobotomy,
and who were given instead the concrete void of insulin
   Metrazol electricity hydrotherapy psychotherapy occupa-
   tional therapy pingpong & amnesia,
who in humorless protest overturned only one symbolic pingpong table, resting briefly in catatonia,

returning years later truly bald except for a wig of blood, and tears and fingers, to the visible madman doom of the wards of the madtowns of the East,

Pilgrim State's Rockland's and Greystone's foetid halls, bickering with the echoes of the soul, rocking and rolling in the midnight solitude-bench dolmen-realms of love, dream of life a nightmare, bodies turned to stone as heavy as the moon,

with mother finally ******, and the last fantastic book flung out of the tenement window, and the last door closed at 4 A.M. and the last telephone slammed at the wall in reply and the last furnished room emptied down to the last piece of mental furniture, a yellow paper rose twisted on a wire hanger in the closet, and even that imaginary, nothing but a hopeful little bit of hallucination –

ah, Carl, while you are not safe I am not safe, and now you're really in the total animal soup of time –

and who therefore ran through the icy streets obsessed with a sudden flash of the alchemy of the use of the ellipse the catalog the meter & the vibrating plane,

who dreamt and made incarnate gaps in Time & Space through images juxtaposed, and trapped the archangel of the soul between 2 visual images and joined the elemental verbs and set the noun and dash of consciousness together jumping with sensation of Pater Omnipotens Aeterna Deus

to recreate the syntax and measure of poor human prose and stand before you speechless and intelligent and shaking with shame, rejected yet confessing out the soul to conform to the rhythm of thought in his naked and endless head,

the madman bum and angel beat in Time, unknown, yet putting down here what might be left to say in time come after death,

and rose reincarnate in the ghostly clothes of jazz in the goldhorn shadow of the band and blew the suffering of America's naked mind for love into an eli eli lamma

lamma sabacthani saxophone cry that shivered the cities
    down to the last radio
with the absolute heart of the poem of life butchered out of
    their own bodies good to eat a thousand years.

II

What sphinx of cement and aluminum bashed open their skulls
    and ate up their brains and imagination?
Moloch! Solitude! Filth! Ugliness! Ashcans and unobtainable
    dollars! Children screaming under the stairways! Boys
    sobbing in armies! Old men weeping in the parks!
Moloch! Moloch! Nightmare of Moloch! Moloch the loveless!
    Mental Moloch! Moloch the heavy judger of men!
Moloch the incomprehensible prison! Moloch the crossbone
    soulless jail-house and Congress of sorrows! Moloch
    whose buildings are judgment! Moloch the vast stone of
    war! Moloch the stunned governments!
Moloch whose mind is pure machinery! Moloch whose blood
    is running money! Moloch whose fingers are ten armies!
    Moloch whose breast is a cannibal dynamo! Moloch
    whose ear is a smoking tomb!
Moloch whose eyes are a thousand blind windows! Moloch
    whose skyscrapers stand in the long streets like endless
    Jehovahs! Moloch whose factories dream and croak in the
    fog! Moloch whose smokestacks and antennae crown the
    cities!
Moloch whose love is endless oil and stone! Moloch whose soul
    is electricity and banks! Moloch whose poverty is the
    specter of genius! Moloch whose fate is a cloud of sexless
    hydrogen! Moloch whose name is the Mind!
Moloch in whom I sit lonely! Moloch in whom I dream Angels!
    Crazy in Moloch! Cocksucker in Moloch! Lacklove and
    manless in Moloch!
Moloch who entered my soul early! Moloch in whom I am a
    consciousness without a body! Moloch who frightened me

out of my natural ecstasy! Moloch whom I abandon! Wake
up in Moloch! Light streaming out of the sky!
Moloch! Moloch! Robot apartments! invisible suburbs! skeleton
treasuries! blind capitals! demonic industries! spectral
nations! invincible mad-houses! granite cocks! monstrous
bombs!
They broke their backs lifting Moloch to Heaven! Pavements,
trees, radios, tons! lifting the city to Heaven which exists
and is everywhere about us!
Visions! omens! hallucinations! miracles! ecstasies! gone down
the American river!
Dreams! adorations! illuminations! religions! the whole boatload
of sensitive bullshit!
Breakthroughs! over the river! flips and crucifixions! gone
down the flood! Highs! Epiphanies! Despairs! Ten years'
animal screams and suicides! Minds! New loves! Mad
generation! down on the rocks of Time!
Real holy laughter in the river! They saw it all! the wild eyes! the
holy yells! They bade farewell! They jumped off the roof!
to solitude! waving! carrying flowers! Down to the river!
into the street!

III

Carl Solomon! I'm with you in Rockland
        where you're madder than I am
I'm with you in Rockland
        where you must feel very strange
I'm with you in Rockland
        where you imitate the shade of my mother
I'm with you in Rockland
        where you've murdered your twelve secretaries
I'm with you in Rockland
        where you laugh at this invisible humor
I'm with you in Rockland
        where we are great writers on the same dreadful typewriter

I'm with you in Rockland
> where your condition has become serious and is reported
> on the radio

I'm with you in Rockland
> where the faculties of the skull no longer admit the worms
> of the senses

I'm with you in Rockland
> where you drink the tea of the breasts of the spinsters of
> Utica

I'm with you in Rockland
> where you pun on the bodies of your nurses the harpies of
> the Bronx

I'm with you in Rockland
> where you scream in a straightjacket that you're losing the
> game of the actual pingpong of the abyss

I'm with you in Rockland
> where you bang on the catatonic piano the soul is innocent
> and immortal it should never die ungodly in an armed
> madhouse

I'm with you in Rockland
> where fifty more shocks will never return your soul to its
> body again from its pilgrimage to a cross in the void

I'm with you in Rockland
> where you accuse your doctors of insanity and plot the
> Hebrew socialist revolution against the fascist national
> Golgotha

I'm with you in Rockland
> where you will split the heavens of Long Island and resur-
> rect your living human Jesus from the superhuman tomb

I'm with you in Rockland
> where there are twentyfive thousand mad comrades all
> together singing the final stanzas of the Internationale

I'm with you in Rockland
> where we hug and kiss the United States under our
> bedsheets the United States that coughs all night and won't
> let us sleep

I'm with you in Rockland
> where we wake up electrified out of the coma by our own
> souls' airplanes roaring over the roof they've come to drop
> angelic bombs the hospital illuminates itself imaginary
> walls collapse O skinny legions run outside O starry-
> spangled shock of mercy the eternal war is here O victory
> forget your underwear we're free

I'm with you in Rockland
> in my dreams you walk dripping from a sea-journey on the
> highway across America in tears to the door of my cottage
> in the Western night

San Francisco, 1955–1956

Footnote to Howl

Holy! Holy! Holy! Holy! Holy! Holy! Holy! Holy! Holy! Holy!
    Holy! Holy! Holy! Holy! Holy!

The world is holy! The soul is holy! The skin is holy! The nose
    is holy! The tongue and cock and hand and asshole holy!

Everything is holy! everybody's holy! everywhere is holy! every-
    day is in eternity! Everyman's an angel!

The bum's as holy as the seraphim! the madman is holy as you
    my soul are holy!

The typewriter is holy the poem is holy the voice is holy the
    hearers are holy the ecstasy is holy!

Holy Peter holy Allen holy Solomon holy Lucien holy Kerouac
    holy Huncke holy Burroughs holy Cassady holy the
    unknown buggered and suffering beggars holy the
    hideous human angels!

Holy my mother in the insane asylum! Holy the cocks of the
    grandfathers of Kansas!

Holy the groaning saxophone! Holy the bop apocalypse! Holy
    the jazzbands marijuana hipsters peace peyote pipes &
    drums!

Holy the solitudes of skyscrapers and pavements! Holy the cafe-
    terias filled with the millions! Holy the mysterious rivers
    of tears under the streets!

Holy the lone juggernaut! Holy the vast lamb of the middle-
    class! Holy the crazy shepherds of rebellion! Who digs Los
    Angeles IS Los Angeles!

Holy New York Holy San Francisco Holy Peoria & Seattle Holy
    Paris Holy Tangiers Holy Moscow Holy Istanbul!

Holy time in eternity holy eternity in time holy the clocks in
    space holy the fourth dimension holy the fifth International
    holy the Angel in Moloch!

Holy the sea holy the desert holy the railroad holy the locomo-
    tive holy the visions holy the hallucinations holy the
    miracles holy the eyeball holy the abyss!

Holy forgiveness! mercy! charity! faith! Holy! Ours! bodies! suf-
     fering! magnanimity!
Holy the supernatural extra brilliant intelligent kindness of the
     soul!

Berkeley, 1955

A Strange New Cottage in Berkeley

All afternoon cutting bramble blackberries off a tottering
brown fence
under a low branch with its rotten old apricots miscella-
neous under the leaves,
fixing the drip in the intricate gut machinery of a new
toilet;
found a good coffeepot in the vines by the porch, rolled a
big tire out of the scarlet bushes, hid my marijuana;
wet the flowers, playing the sunlit water each to each,
returning for godly extra drops for the stringbeans and daisies;
three times walked round the grass and sighed absently:
my reward, when the garden fed me its plums from the
form of a small tree in the corner,
an angel thoughtful of my stomach, and my dry and
lovelorn tongue.

1955

A Supermarket in California

What thoughts I have of you tonight, Walt Whitman, for I walked down the sidestreets under the trees with a headache self-conscious looking at the full moon.

In my hungry fatigue, and shopping for images, I went into the neon fruit supermarket, dreaming of your enumerations!

What peaches and what penumbras! Whole families shopping at night! Aisles full of husbands! Wives in the avocados, babies in the tomatoes! – and you, García Lorca, what were you doing down by the watermelons?

I saw you, Walt Whitman, childless, lonely old grubber, poking among the meats in the refrigerator and eyeing the grocery boys.

I heard you asking questions of each: Who killed the pork chops? What price bananas? Are you my Angel?

I wandered in and out of the brilliant stacks of cans following you, and followed in my imagination by the store detective.

We strode down the open corridors together in our solitary fancy tasting artichokes, possessing every frozen delicacy, and never passing the cashier.

Where are we going, Walt Whitman? The doors close in an hour. Which way does your beard point tonight?

(I touch your book and dream of our odyssey in the supermarket and feel absurd.)

Will we walk all night through solitary streets? The trees add shade to shade, lights out in the houses, we'll both be lonely.

Will we stroll dreaming of the lost America of love past blue automobiles in driveways, home to our silent cottage?

Ah, dear father, graybeard, lonely old courage-teacher, what America did you have when Charon quit poling his ferry and you got out on a smoking bank and stood watching the boat disappear on the black waters of Lethe?

Berkeley, 1955

Sunflower Sutra

I walked on the banks of the tincan banana dock and sat down
under the huge shade of a Southern Pacific locomotive to
look at the sunset over the box house hills and cry.
Jack Kerouac sat beside me on a busted rusty iron pole, companion, we thought the same thoughts of the soul, bleak
and blue and sad-eyed, surrounded by the gnarled steel
roots of trees of machinery.
The oily water on the river mirrored the red sky, sun sank on top
of final Frisco peaks, no fish in that stream, no hermit in
those mounts, just ourselves rheumy-eyed and hung-over
like old bums on the river-bank, tired and wily.
Look at the Sunflower, he said, there was a dead gray shadow
against the sky, big as a man, sitting dry on top of a pile of
ancient sawdust –
– I rushed up enchanted – it was my first sunflower, memories
of Blake – my visions – Harlem
and Hells of the Eastern rivers, bridges clanking Joes Greasy
Sandwiches, dead baby carriages, black treadless tires forgotten and unretreaded, the poem of the riverbank, con-
doms & pots, steel knives, nothing stainless, only the dank
muck and the razor-sharp artifacts passing into the past –
and the gray Sunflower poised against the sunset, crackly bleak
and dusty with the smut and smog and smoke of olden
locomotives in its eye –
corolla of bleary spikes pushed down and broken like a battered
crown, seeds fallen out of its face, soon-to-be-toothless
mouth of sunny air, sunrays obliterated on its hairy head
like a dried wire spiderweb,
leaves stuck out like arms out of the stem, gestures from the
sawdust root, broke pieces of plaster fallen out of the black
twigs, a dead fly in its ear,
Unholy battered old thing you were, my sunflower O my soul,
I loved you then!

The grime was no man's grime but death and human
   locomotives,
all that dress of dust, that veil of darkened railroad skin, that
   smog of cheek, that eyelid of black mis'ry, that sooty hand
   or phallus or protuberance of artificial worse-than-dirt –
   industrial – modern – all that civilization spotting your
   crazy golden crown –
and those blear thoughts of death and dusty loveless eyes and
   ends and withered roots below, in the home-pile of sand
   and sawdust, rubber dollar bills, skin of machinery, the
   guts and innards of the weeping coughing car, the empty
   lonely tincans with their rusty tongues alack, what more
   could I name, the smoked ashes of some cock cigar, the
   cunts of wheelbarrows and the milky breasts of cars,
   wornout asses out of chairs & sphincters of dynamos – all
   these
entangled in your mummied roots – and you there standing
   before me in the sunset, all your glory in your form!
A perfect beauty of a sunflower! a perfect excellent lovely sunflower existence! a sweet natural eye to the new hip moon,
   woke up alive and excited grasping in the sunset shadow
   sunrise golden monthly breeze!
How many flies buzzed round you innocent of your grime,
   while you cursed the heavens of the railroad and your
   flower soul?
Poor dead flower? when did you forget you were a flower? when
   did you look at your skin and decide you were an impo-
   tent dirty old locomotive? the ghost of a locomotive? the
   specter and shade of a once powerful mad American
   locomotive?
You were never no locomotive, Sunflower, you were a sunflower!
And you Locomotive, you are a locomotive, forget me not!
So I grabbed up the skeleton thick sunflower and stuck it at my
   side like a scepter,

and deliver my sermon to my soul, and Jack's soul too, and anyone who'll listen,
– We're not our skin of grime, we're not our dread bleak dusty
imageless locomotive, we're all golden sunflowers inside,
blessed by our own seed & hairy naked accomplishment-
bodies growing into mad black formal sunflowers in the
sunset, spied on by our eyes under the shadow of the mad
locomotive riverbank sunset Frisco hilly tincan evening
sitdown vision.

Berkeley, 1955

Sather Gate Illumination

Why do I deny manna to another?
Because I deny it to myself.
Why have I denied myself?
What other has rejected me?
Now I believe you are lovely, my soul, soul of Allen, Allen –
and you so beloved, so sweetened, so recalled to your true
      loveliness,
your original nude breathing Allen
will you ever deny another again?

Dear Walter, thanks for the message
I forbid you not to touch me, man to man, True American.

The bombers jet through the sky in unison of twelve,
the pilots are sweating and nervous at the controls in the hot
      cabins.
Over what souls will they loose their loveless bombs?

The Campanile pokes its white granite (?) innocent head into
      the clouds for me to look at.

A cripple lady explains French grammar with a loud sweet
      voice: Regarder is to look –
the whole French language looks on the trees on the campus.

      The girls' haunted voices make quiet dates for 2 o'clock –
yet one of them waves farewell and smiles at last – her red
skirt swinging shows how she loves herself.

      Another encased in flashy Scotch clothes clomps up the
concrete in a hurry – into the door – poor dear! – who will
receive you in love's offices?

How many beautiful boys have I seen on this spot?
The trees seem on the verge of moving – ah! they do move in
      the breeze.
Roar again of airplanes in the sky – everyone looks up.

And do you know that all these rubbings of the eyes & painful
     gestures to the brow
of suited scholars entering Dwinelle (Hall) are Holy Signs? –
     anxiety and fear?
How many years have I got to float on this sweetened scene of
     trees & humans clomping above ground –
O I must be mad to sit here lonely in the void & glee & build
     up thoughts of love!
But what do I have to doubt but my own shiny eyes, what to
     lose but life which is a vision today this afternoon.

     My stomach is light, I relax, new sentences spring forth
out of the scene to describe spontaneous forms of Time –
trees, sleeping dogs, airplanes wandering thru the air, negroes
with their lunch books of anxiety, apples and sandwiches,
lunchtime, icecream, Timeless –

And even the ugliest will seek beauty – 'What are you doing
     Friday night?'
asks the sailor in white school training cap & gilt buttons &
     blue coat,
and the little ape in a green jacket and baggy pants and
     overloaded school-book satchel says 'Quartets.'
Every Friday nite, beautiful quartets to celebrate and please
     my soul with all its hair – Music!
and then strides off, snapping pieces chocolate off a bar
     wrapped in Hershey brown paper and tinfoil,
eating chocolate rose.

& how can those other boys be them happy selves in their
     brown army study uniforms?

Now cripple girl swings down walk with loping fuck gestures
     of her hips askew –
let her roll her eyes in abandon & camp angelic through the
     campus bouncing her body about in joy –
someone will dig that pelvic energy for sure.

Those white stripes down your chocolate cupcake, Lady (held
        in front of your nose finishing sentence preparatory to
        chomp),
they were painted there to delight you by some spanish
        industrial artistic hand in bakery factory faraway,
expert hand in simple-minded messages of white stripes on
        millions of message cupcakes.
I have a message for you all – I will denote one particularity of
        each!

        And there goes Professor Hart striding enlightened by
the years through the doorway and arcade he built (in his
mind) and knows – he too saw the ruins of Yucatán once –

followed by a lonely janitor in dovegray italian fruitpeddler
        Chico Marx hat pushing his rolypoly belly thru the trees.

N sees all girls
as visions of
their inner cunts,
yes, it's true!
and all men walking
along thinking
of their spirit cocks.

So look at that poor dread boy
with two-day black hair
all over his dirty face,
how he must hate his cock
        – Chinamen stop shuddering

        and now to bring this to an end with a rise and an
ellipse –

        The boys are now all talking to the girls 'If I was a girl I'd
love all boys' & girls giggling the opposite, all pretty
everywhichway
and even I have my secret beds and lovers under another
        moonlight, be you sure

& any minute I expect to see a baby carriage pushed on to the
    scene
and everyone turn in attention like the airplanes and laughter,
    like a Greek Campus
and the big brown shaggy silent dog lazing openeyed in the
    shade
lift up his head & sniff & lower his head on his golden paws &
    let his belly rumble away unconcerned.

    . . . the lion's ruddy eyes
Shall flow with tears of gold.

Now the silence is broken, students pour onto the square, the
    doors are crowded, the dog gets up and walks away,
the cripple swings out of Dwinelle, a nun even, I wonder
    about her, an old lady distinguished by a cane,
we all look up, silence moves, huge changes upon the ground,
    and in the air thoughts fly all over, filling space.

My grief at Peter's not loving me was grief at not loving
    myself.
Huge Karmas of broken minds in beautiful bodies unable to
    receive love because not knowing the self as lovely –
Fathers and Teachers!

    Seeing in people the visible evidence of inner self
thought by their treatment of me: who loves himself loves me
who love myself.

Berkeley, September 1955

America

America I've given you all and now I'm nothing.
America two dollars and twentyseven cents January 17, 1956.
I can't stand my own mind.
America when will we end the human war?
Go fuck yourself with your atom bomb.
I don't feel good don't bother me.
I won't write my poem till I'm in my right mind.
America when will you be angelic?
When will you take off your clothes?
When will you look at yourself through the grave?
When will you be worthy of your million Trotskyites?
America why are your libraries full of tears?
America when will you send your eggs to India?
I'm sick of your insane demands.
When can I go into the supermarket and buy what I need with
    my good looks?
America after all it is you and I who are perfect not the next
    world.
Your machinery is too much for me.
You made me want to be a saint.
There must be some other way to settle this argument.
Burroughs is in Tangiers I don't think he'll come back it's
    sinister.
Are you being sinister or is this some form of practical joke?
I'm trying to come to the point.
I refuse to give up my obsession.
America stop pushing I know what I'm doing.
America the plum blossoms are falling.
I haven't read the newspapers for months, everyday somebody
    goes on trial for murder.
America I feel sentimental about the Wobblies.
America I used to be a communist when I was a kid I'm not
    sorry.

I smoke marijuana every chance I get.

I sit in my house for days on end and stare at the roses in the closet.

When I go to Chinatown I get drunk and never get laid.

My mind is made up there's going to be trouble.

You should have seen me reading Marx.

My psychoanalyst thinks I'm perfectly right.

I won't say the Lord's Prayer.

I have mystical visions and cosmic vibrations.

America I still haven't told you what you did to Uncle Max after he came over from Russia.

I'm addressing you.

Are you going to let your emotional life be run by Time Magazine?

I'm obsessed by Time Magazine.

I read it every week.

Its cover stares at me every time I slink past the corner candystore.

I read it in the basement of the Berkeley Public Library.

It's always telling me about responsibility. Businessmen are serious. Movie producers are serious. Everybody's serious but me.

It occurs to me that I am America.

I am talking to myself again.

Asia is rising against me.

I haven't got a chinaman's chance.

I'd better consider my national resources.

My national resources consist of two joints of marijuana millions of genitals an unpublishable private literature that jetplanes 1400 miles an hour and twentyfive-thousand mental institutions.

I say nothing about my prisons nor the millions of underprivileged who live in my flowerpots under the light of five hundred suns.

I have abolished the whorehouses of France, Tangiers is the next to go.

My ambition is to be President despite the fact that I'm a
  Catholic.

America how can I write a holy litany in your silly mood?
I will continue like Henry Ford my strophes are as individual as
  his automobiles more so they're all different sexes.
America I will sell you strophes $2500 apiece $500 down on
  your old strophe
America free Tom Mooney
America save the Spanish Loyalists
America Sacco & Vanzetti must not die
America I am the Scottsboro boys.
America when I was seven momma took me to Communist Cell
  meetings they sold us garbanzos a handful per ticket a ticket
  costs a nickel and the speeches were free everybody was
  angelic and sentimental about the workers it was all so
  sincere you have no idea what a good thing the party was
  in 1835 Scott Nearing was a grand old man a real mensch
  Mother Bloor the Silk-strikers' Ewig-Weibliche made me
  cry I once saw the Yiddish orator Israel Amter plain.
  Everybody must have been a spy.
America you don't really want to go to war.
America it's them bad Russians.
Them Russians them Russians and them Chinamen. And them
  Russians.
The Russia wants to eat us alive. The Russia's power mad. She
  wants to take our cars from out our garages.
Her wants to grab Chicago. Her needs a Red *Reader's Digest*.
  Her wants our auto plants in Siberia. Him big bureaucracy
  running our fillingstations.
That no good. Ugh. Him make Indians learn read. Him need
  big black niggers. Hah. Her make us all work sixteen hours
  a day. Help.
America this is quite serious.
America this is the impression I get from looking in the tele-
  vision set.

America is this correct?

I'd better get right down to the job.

It's true I don't want to join the Army or turn lathes in precision parts factories, I'm nearsighted and psychopathic
anyway.

America I'm putting my queer shoulder to the wheel.

Berkeley, January 17, 1956

Psalm III

To God: to illuminate all men. Beginning with Skid Road.

Let Occidental and Washington be transformed into a higher place, the plaza of eternity.

Illuminate the welders in shipyards with the brilliance of their torches.

Let the crane operator lift up his arm for joy.

Let elevators creak and speak, ascending and descending in awe.

Let the mercy of the flower's direction beckon in the eye.

Let the straight flower bespeak its purpose in straightness – to seek the light.

Let the crooked flower bespeak its purpose in crookedness – to seek the light.

Let the crookedness and straightness bespeak the light.

Let Puget Sound be a blast of light.

I feed on your Name like a cockroach on a crumb – this cockroach is holy.

Seattle, June, 1956

Many Loves

'Resolved to sing no songs henceforth but those of manly attachment'

— Walt Whitman

Neal Cassady was my animal: he brought me to my knees
and taught me the love of his cock and the secrets of his mind
And we met and conversed, went walking in the evening by the
    park
Up to Harlem, recollecting Denver, and Dan Budd, a hero
And we made shift to sack out in Harlem, after a long evening,
Jack and host in a large double bed, I volunteered for the cot,
    and Neal
Volunteered for the cot with me, we stripped and lay down.
I wore my underwear, my shorts, and he his briefs –
lights out on the narrow bed I turned to my side, with my back
    to his Irish boy's torso,
and huddled and balanced on the edge, and kept distance –
and hung my head over and kept my arm over the side, with-
    drawn
And he seeing my fear stretched out his arm, and put it around
    my breast
Saying 'Draw near me' and gathered me in upon him:
I lay there trembling, and felt his great arm like a king's
And his breasts, his heart slow thudding against my back,
and his middle torso, narrow and made of iron, soft at my back,
his fiery firm belly warming me while I trembled –
His belly of fists and starvation, his belly a thousand girls kissed
    in Colorado
his belly of rocks thrown over Denver roofs, prowess of jump-
    ing and fists, his stomach of solitudes,
His belly of burning iron and jails affectionate to my side:
I began to tremble, he pulled me in closer with his arm, and
    hugged me long and close
my soul melted, secrecy departed, I became

33

Thenceforth open to his nature as a flower in the shining sun.

And below his belly, in white underwear, tight between my buttocks,

His own loins against me soft, nestling in comradeship, put forth & pressed into me, open to my awareness,

slowly began to grow, signal me further and deeper affection, sexual tenderness.

So gentle the man, so sweet the moment, so kind the thighs that nuzzled against me smooth-skinned powerful, warm by my legs

That my body shudders and trembles with happiness, remembering –

His hand opened up on my belly, his palms and fingers flat against my skin

I fell to him, and turned, shifting, put my face on his arm resting,

my chest against his, he helped me to turn, and held me closer

his arm at my back beneath my head, and arm at my buttocks tender holding me in,

our bellies together nestling, loins touched together, pressing and knowledgeable each other's hardness, and mine stuck out of my underwear.

Then I pressed in closer and drew my leg up between his, and he lay half on me with his thighs and bedded me down close, caressing

and moved together pressing his cock to my thigh and mine to his

slowly, and slowly began a love match that continues in my imagination to this day a full decade.

Thus I met Neal & thus we felt each other's flesh and owned each other bodies and souls.

So then as I lay on his breast with my arms clasped around his neck and his cheek against mine,

I put my hand down to feel his great back for the first time, jaws and pectorals of steel at my fingers,

closer and stiller, down the silken iron back to his waist, the
whole of his torso now open

my hand at his waist trembling, waited delaying and under the
elastic of his briefs,

I first touched the smooth mount of his rock buttocks, silken in
power, rounded in animal fucking and bodily nights over
nurses and schoolgirls,

O ass of long solitudes in stolen cars, and solitudes on curbs,
musing fist in cheek,

Ass of a thousand farewells, ass of youth, youth's lovers,

Ass of a thousand lonely craps in gas stations ass of great
painful secrecies of the years

O ass of mystery and night! ass of gymnasiums and muscular
pants

ass of high schools and masturbation ass of lone delight, ass of
mankind, so beautiful and hollow, dowry of Mind and
Angels,

Ass of hero, Neal Cassady, I had at my hand: my fingers traced
the curve to the bottom of his thighs.

I raised my thighs and stripped down my shorts to my knees,
and bent to push them off

and he raised me up from his chest, and pulled down his pants
the same,

humble and meek and obedient to his mood our silence,

and naked at long last with angel & greek & athlete & hero and
brother and boy of my dreams

I lay with my hair intermixed with his, he asking me 'What shall
we do now?'

– And confessed, years later, he thinking I was not a queer at
first to please me & serve me, to blow me and make me
come, maybe or if I were queer, that's what I'd likely want
of a dumb bastard like him.

But I made my first mistake, and made him then and there
my master, and bowed my head, and holding his
buttock

Took up his hard-on and held it, feeling it throb and pressing
 my own at his knee & breathing showed him I needed him,
 cock, for my dreams of insatiety & lone love.

– And I lie here naked in the dark, dreaming

Arctic, August 10, 1956

Death to Van Gogh's Ear!

POET is Priest
Money has reckoned the soul of America
Congress broken thru to the precipice of Eternity
the President built a War machine which will vomit and rear up
    Russia out of Kansas
The American Century betrayed by a mad Senate which no
    longer sleeps with its wife
Franco has murdered Lorca the fairy son of Whitman
just as Mayakovsky committed suicide to avoid Russia
Hart Crane distinguished Platonist committed suicide to cave
    in the wrong America
just as milions of tons of human wheat were burned in secret
    caverns under the White House
while India starved and screamed and ate mad dogs full of
    rain
and mountains of eggs were reduced to white powder in the
    halls of Congress
no godfearing man will walk there again because of the stink of
    the rotten eggs of America
and the Indians of Chiapas continue to gnaw their vitaminless
    tortillas
aborigines of Australia perhaps gibber in the eggless wilderness
and I rarely have an egg for breakfast tho my work requires
    infinite eggs to come to birth in Eternity
eggs should be eaten or given to their mothers
and the grief of the countless chickens of America is expressed
    in the screaming of her comedians over the radio
Detroit has built a million automobiles of rubber trees and
    phantoms
but I walk, I walk, and the Orient walks with me, and all Africa
    walks
and sooner or later North America will walk

for as we have driven the Chinese Angel from our door he will
　　　drive us from the Golden Door of the future
we have not cherished pity on Tanganyika
Einstein alive was mocked for his heavenly politics
Bertrand Russell driven from New York for getting laid
immortal Chaplin driven from our shores with the rose in his
　　　teeth
a secret conspiracy by Catholic Church in the lavatories of
　　　Congress has denied contraceptives to the unceasing
　　　masses of India.
Nobody publishes a word that is not the cowardly robot ravings
　　　of a depraved mentality
The day of the publication of the true literature of the
　　　American body will be day of Revolution
the revolution of the sexy lamb
the only bloodless revolution that gives away corn
poor Genet will illuminate the harvesters of Ohio
Marijuana is a benevolent narcotic but J. Edgar Hoover prefers
　　　his deathly scotch
And the heroin of Lao-Tze & the Sixth Patriarch is punished by
　　　the electric chair
but the poor sick junkies have nowhere to lay their heads
fiends in our government have invented a cold-turkey cure for
　　　addiction as obsolete as the Defense Early Warning Radar
　　　System.
I am the defense early warning radar system
I see nothing but bombs
I am not interested in preventing Asia from being Asia
and the governments of Russia and Asia will rise and fall but
　　　Asia and Russia will not fall
the government of America also will fall but how can America
　　　fall
I doubt if anyone will ever fall anymore except governments
fortunately all the governments will fall
the only ones which won't fall are the good ones
and the good ones don't yet exist

But they have to begin existing they exist in my poems
they exist in the death of the Russian and American govern-
      ments
they exist in the death of Hart Crane & Mayakovsky
Now is the time for prophecy without death as a consequence
the universe will ultimately disappear
Hollywood will rot on the windmills of Eternity
Hollywood whose movies stick in the throat of God
Yes Hollywood will get what it deserves
Time
Seepage of nerve-gas over the radio
History will make this poem prophetic and its awful silliness a
      hideous spiritual music
I have the moan of doves and the feather of ecstasy
Man cannot long endure the hunger of the cannibal abstract
War is abstract
the world will be destroyed
but I will die only for poetry, that will save the world
Monument to Sacco & Vanzetti not yet financed to ennoble
      Boston
natives of Kenya tormented by idiot con-men from England
South Africa in the grip of the white fool
Vachel Lindsay Secretary of the Interior
Poe Secretary of Imagination
Pound Secty. Economics
and Kra belongs to Kra, and Pukti to Pukti
crossfertilization of Blok and Artaud
Van Gogh's Ear on the currency
no more propaganda for monsters
and poets should stay out of politics or become monsters
I have become monsterous with politics
the Russian poet undoubtedly monsterous in his secret note-
      book
Tibet should be left alone
These are obvious prophecies
America will be destroyed

Russian poets will struggle with Russia

Whitman warned against this 'fabled Damned of nations'

Where was Theodore Roosevelt when he sent out ultimatums from his castle in Camden

Where was the House of Representatives when Crane read aloud from his prophetic books

What was Wall Street scheming when Lindsay announced the doom of Money

Were they listening to my ravings in the locker rooms of Bickfords Employment Offices?

Did they bend their ears to the moans of my soul when I struggled with market research statistics in the Forum at Rome?

No they were fighting in fiery offices, on carpets of heartfailure, screaming and bargaining with Destiny

fighting the Skeleton with sabers, muskets, buck teeth, indigestion, bombs of larceny, whoredom, rockets, pederasty,

back to the wall to build up their wives and apartments, lawns, suburbs, fairydoms,

Puerto Ricans crowded for massacre on 114th St. for the sake of an imitation Chinese-Moderne refrigerator

Elephants of mercy murdered for the sake of an Elizabethan birdcage

millions of agitated fanatics in the bughouse for the sake of the screaming soprano of industry

Money-chant of soapers – toothpaste apes in television sets – deodorizers on hypnotic chairs –

petroleum mongers in Texas – jet plane streaks among the clouds –

sky writers liars in the face of Divinity – fanged butchers of hats and shoes, all Owners! Owners! Owners! with obsession on property and vanishing Selfhood!

and their long editorials on the fence of the screaming negro attacked by ants crawled out of the front page!

Machinery of a mass electrical dream! A war-creating Whore of Babylon bellowing over Capitols and Academies!

Money! Money! Money! shrieking mad celestial money of
   illusion! Money made of nothing, starvation, suicide!
   Money of failure! Money of death!
Money against Eternity! and eternity's strong mills grind
   out vast paper of Illusion!

Paris, December 1957

The Lion for Real

'Soyez muette pour moi, Idole contemplative . . .'

I came home and found a lion in my living room
Rushed out on the fire escape screaming Lion! Lion!
Two stenographers pulled their brunette hair and banged the
    window shut
I hurried home to Paterson and stayed two days.

Called up my old Reichian analyst
who'd kicked me out of therapy for smoking marijuana
'It's happened' I panted 'There's a Lion in my room'
'I'm afraid any discussion would have no value' he hung up.

I went to my old boyfriend we got drunk with his girlfriend
I kissed him and announced I had a lion with a mad gleam in
    my eye
We wound up fighting on the floor I bit his eyebrow & he
    kicked me out
I ended masturbating in his jeep parked in the street moaning
    'Lion.'

Found Joey my novelist friend and roared at him 'Lion!'
He looked at me interested and read me his spontaneous ignu
    high poetries
I listened for lions all I heard was Elephant Tiglon Hippogriff
    Unicorn Ants
But figured he really understood me when we made it in Ignaz
    Wisdom's bathroom.

But next day he sent me a leaf from his Smoky Mountain retreat
'I love you little Bo-Bo with your delicate golden lions
But there being no Self and No Bars therefore the Zoo of your
    dear Father hath no Lion
You said your mother was mad don't expect me to produce the
    Monster for your Bridegroom.'

Confused dazed and exalted bethought me of real lion starved
in his stink in Harlem
Opened the door the room was filled with the bomb blast of his
anger
He roaring hungrily at the plaster walls but nobody could hear
him outside thru the window
My eye caught the edge of the red neighbor apartment building
standing in deafening stillness

We gazed at each other his implacable yellow eye in the red halo
of fur
Waxed rheumy on my own but he stopped roaring and bared a
fang greeting.
I turned my back and cooked broccoli for supper on an iron gas
stove
boilt water and took a hot bath in the old tub under the sink
board.

He didn't eat me, tho I regretted him starving in my presence.
Next week he wasted away a sick rug full of bones wheaten hair
falling out
enraged and reddening eye as he lay aching huge hairy head on
his paws
by the egg-crate bookcase filled up with thin volumes of Plato,
& Buddha.

Sat by his side every night averting my eyes from his hungry
motheaten face
stopped eating myself he got weaker and roared at night while
I had nightmares
Eaten by lion in bookstore on Cosmic Campus, a lion myself
starved by Professor Kandisky, dying in a lion's flophouse
circus,
I woke up mornings the lion still added dying on the floor –
'Terrible Presence!' I cried 'Eat me or die!'

It got up that afternoon – walked to the door with its paw on
the wall to steady its trembling body

Let out a soul-rending creak from the bottomless roof of his
   mouth
thundering from my floor to heaven heavier than a volcano at
   night in Mexico
Pushed the door open and said in a gravelly voice 'Not this time
   Baby – but I will be back again.'

Lion that eats my mind now for a decade knowing only your
   hunger
Not the bliss of your satisfaction O roar of the Universe how am
   I chosen
In this life I have heard your promise I am ready to die I have
   served
Your starved and ancient Presence O Lord I wait in my room at
   your Mercy.

Paris, March 1958

At Apollinaire's Grave

'... *voici le temps*
Où l'on connaîtra l'avenir
Sans mourir de connaissance'

I

I visited Père Lachaise to look for the remains of Apollinaire
the day the U.S. President appeared in France for the grand con-
    ference of heads of state
so let it be the airport at blue Orly a springtime clarity in the air
    over Paris
Eisenhower winging in from his American graveyard
and over the froggy graves at Père Lachaise an illusory mist as
    thick as marijuana smoke
Peter Orlovsky and I walked softly thru Père Lachaise we both
    knew we would die
and so held temporary hands tenderly in a citylike miniature
    eternity
roads and streetsigns rocks and hills and names on everybody's
    house
looking for the lost address of a notable Frenchman of the
    Void
to pay our tender crime of homage to his helpless menhir
and lay my temporary American Howl on top of his silent
    Calligramme
for him to read between the lines with Xray eyes of Poet
as he by miracle had read his own death lyric in the Seine
I hope some wild kidmonk lays his pamphlet on my grave for
    God to read me on cold winter nights in heaven
already our hands have vanished from that place my hand
    writes now in a room in Paris Git-le-Coeur
Ah William what grit in the brain you had what's death
I walked all over the cemetery and still couldn't find your grave
what did you mean by that fantastic cranial bandage in your
    poems

O solemn stinking deathshead what've you got to say nothing
and that's barely an answer

You can't drive autos into a sixfoot grave tho the universe is
mausoleum big enough for anything
the universe is a graveyard and I walk around alone in here
knowing that Apollinaire was on the same street 50 years ago
his madness is only around the corner and Genet is with us
stealing books
the West is at war again and whose lucid suicide will set it all
right
Guillaume Guillaume how I envy your fame your accomplish-
ment for American letters
your Zone with its long crazy line of bullshit about death
come out of the grave and talk thru the door of my mind
issue new series of images oceanic haikus blue taxicabs in
Moscow negro statues of Buddha
pray for me on the phonograph record of your former existence
with a long sad voice and strophes of deep sweet music sad and
scratchy as World War I
I've eaten the blue carrots you sent out of the grave and Van
Gogh's ear and maniac peyote of Artaud
and will walk down the streets of New York in the black cloak
of French poetry
improvising our conversation in Paris at Père Lachaise
and the future poem that takes its inspiration from the light
bleeding into your grave

II

Here in Paris I am your guest O friendly shade
the absent hand of Max Jacob
Picasso in youth bearing me a tube of Mediterranean
myself attending Rousseau's old red banquet I ate his violin
great party at the Bateau Lavoir not mentioned in the textbooks
of Algeria

Tzara in the Bois de Boulogne explaining the alchemy of the
    machineguns of the cuckoos
he weeps translating me into Swedish
well dressed in a violet tie and black pants
a sweet purple beard which emerged from his face like the moss
    hanging from the walls of Anarchism
he spoke endlessly of his quarrels with André Breton
whom he had helped one day trim his golden mustache
old Blaise Cendrars received me into his study and spoke
    wearily of the enormous length of Siberia
Jacques Vaché invited me to inspect his terrible collection of
    pistols
poor Cocteau saddened by the once marvelous Radiguet at his
    last thought I fainted
Rigaut with a letter of introduction to Death
and Gide praised the telephone and other remarkable inventions
we agreed in principle though he gossiped of lavender underwear
but for all that he drank deeply of the grass of Whitman and
    was intrigued by all lovers named Colorado
princes of America arriving with their armfuls of shrapnel and
    baseball
Oh Guillaume the world so easy to fight seemed so easy
did you know the great political classicists would invade
    Montparnasse
with not one sprig of prophetic laurel to green their foreheads
not one pulse of green in their pillows no leaf left from their
    wars – Mayakovsky arrived and revolted

III

Came back sat on a tomb and stared at your rough menhir
a piece of thin granite like an unfinished phallus
a cross fading into the rock 2 poems on the stone one Coeur
    Renversée
other Habituez-vous comme moi A ces prodiges que j'annonce
    Guillaume Apollinaire de Kostrowitsky

someone placed a jam bottle filled with daisies and a 5&10¢
    surrealist typist ceramic rose
happy little tomb with flowers and overturned heart
under a fine mossy tree beneath which I sat snaky trunk
summer boughs and leaves umbrella over the menhir and
    nobody there
Et quelle voix sinistre ulule Guillaume qu'es-tu devenu
his nextdoor neighbor is a tree
there underneath the crossed bones heaped and yellow cranium
    perhaps
and the printed poems Alcools in my pocket his voice in the
    museum
Now middleage footsteps walk the gravel
a man stares at the name and moves toward the crematory
    building
same sky rolls over thru clouds as Mediterranean days on the
    Riviera during war
drinking Apollo in love eating occasional opium he'd taken the
    light
One must have felt the shock in St. Germain when he went out
    Jacob & Picasso coughing in the dark
a bandage unrolled and the skull left still on a bed outstretched
    pudgy fingers the mystery and ego gone
a bell tolls in the steeple down the street birds warble in the
    chestnut trees
Famille Bremont sleeps nearby Christ hangs big chested and
    sexy in their tomb
my cigarette smokes in my lap and fills the page with smoke and
    flames
an ant runs over my corduroy sleeve the tree I lean on grows
    slowly
bushes and branches upstarting through the tombs one silky
    spiderweb gleaming on granite
I am buried here and sit by my grave beneath a tree

Paris, Winter–Spring 1958

To Lindsay

Vachel, the stars are out
dusk has fallen on the Colorado road
a car crawls slowly across the plain
in the dim light the radio blares its jazz
the heartbroken salesman lights another cigarette
In another city 27 years ago
I see your shadow on the wall
you're sitting in your suspenders on the bed
the shadow hand lifts up a Lysol bottle to your head
your shade falls over on the floor

Paris, May 1958

To Aunt Rose

Aunt Rose – now – might I see you
with your thin face and buck tooth smile and pain
        of rheumatism – and a long black heavy shoe
        for your bony left leg
limping down the long hall in Newark on the running carpet
        past the black grand piano
        in the day room
            where the parties were
      and I sang Spanish loyalist songs
      in a high squeaky voice
         (hysterical) the committee listening
    while you limped around the room
      collected the money –
Aunt Honey, Uncle Sam, a stranger with a cloth arm
      in his pocket
        and huge young bald head
        of Abraham Lincoln Brigade

– your long sad face
    your tears of sexual frustration
      (what smothered sobs and bony hips
        under the pillows of Osborne Terrace)
– the time I stood on the toilet seat naked
    and you powdered my thighs with calamine
    against the poison ivy – my tender
        and shamed first black curled hairs
what were you thinking in secret heart then
    knowing me a man already –
and I an ignorant girl of family silence on the thin pedestal
    of my legs in the bathroom – Museum of Newark.

        Aunt Rose
Hitler is dead, Hitler is in Eternity; Hitler is with
      Tamburlane and Emily Brontë

Though I see you walking still, a ghost on Osborne Terrace
          down the long dark hall to the front door
     limping a little with a pinched smile
        in what must have been a silken
                    flower dress
welcoming my father, the Poet, on his visit to Newark
          – see you arriving in the living room
               dancing on your crippled leg
               and clapping hands his book
                    had been accepted by Liveright

Hitler is dead and Liveright's gone out of business
The Attic of the Past and *Everlasting Minute* are out of print
               Uncle Harry sold his last silk stocking
               Claire quit interpretive dancing school
                    Buba sits a wrinkled monument in Old
                    Ladies Home blinking at new babies

last time I saw you was the hospital
               pale skull protruding under ashen skin
               blue veined unconscious girl
                    in an oxygen tent
          the war in Spain has ended long ago
                    Aunt Rose

                         Paris, June 1958

American Change

The first I looked on, after a long time far from home in mid Atlantic on a summer day

Dolphins breaking the glassy water under the blue sky,

a gleam of silver in my cabin, fished up out of my jangling new pocket of coins and green dollars

– held in my palm, the head of the feathered indian, old Buck-Rogers eagle eyed face, a gash of hunger in the cheek

gritted jaw of the vanished man begone like a Hebrew with hairlock combed down the side – O Rabbi Indian

what visionary gleam 100 years ago on Buffalo prairie under the molten cloud-shot sky, 'the same clear light 10000 miles in all directions'

but now with all the violin music of Vienna, gone into the great slot machine of Kansas City, Reno –

The coin seemed so small after vast European coppers thick francs leaden pesetas, lire endless and heavy,

a miniature primeval memorialized in 5¢ nickel candy-store nostalgia of the redskin, dead on silver coin,

with shaggy buffalo on reverse, hump-backed little tail incurved, head butting against the rondure of Eternity,

cock forelock below, bearded shoulder muscle folded below muscle, head of prophet, bowed,

vanishing beast of Time, hoar body rubbed clean of wrinkles and shining like polished stone, bright metal in my forefinger, ridiculous buffalo – Go to New York.

Dime next I found, Minerva, sexless cold & chill, ascending goddess of money – and was it the wife of Wallace Stevens, truly?

and now from the locks flowing the miniature wings of speedy thought,

executive dyke, Minerva, goddess of Madison Avenue, forgotten useless dime that can't buy hot dog, dead dime –

Then we've George Washington, less primitive, the snub-nosed quarter, smug eyes and mouth, some idiot's design of the sexless Father,

naked down to his neck, a ribbon in his wig, high forehead, Roman line down the nose, fat cheeked, still showing his false-tooth ideas – O Eisenhower & Washington – O Fathers – No movie star dark beauty – O thou Bignoses –

Quarter, remembered quarter, 40¢ in all – What'll you buy me when I land – one icecream soda? –

poor pile of coins, original reminders of the sadness, forgotten money of America –

nostalgia of the first touch of those coins, American change,

the memory in my aging hand, the same old silver reflective there,

the thin dime hidden between my thumb and forefinger

All the struggles for those coins, the sadness of their reappearance

my reappearance on those fabled shores

and the failure of that Dream, that Vision of Money reduced to this haunting recollection

of the gas lot in Paterson where I found half a dollar gleaming in the grass –

I have a $5 bill in my pocket – it's Lincoln's sour black head moled wrinkled, forelocked too, big eared, flags of announcement flying over the bill, stamps in green and spider-web black,

long numbers in racetrack green, immense promise, a girl, a hotel, a busride to Albany, a night of brilliant drunk in some faraway corner of Manhattan

a stick of several teas, or paper or cap of Heroin, or a $5 strange present to the blind.

Money money, reminder, I might as well write poems to you – dear American money – O statue of Liberty I ride enfolded in money in my mind to you – and last

Ahhh! Washington again, on the Dollar, same poetic black print, dark words, The United States of America, innumerable numbers

R956422481 One Dollar This Certificate is Legal Tender (tender!) for all debts public and private

My God My God why have you forsaken me

Ivy Baker Priest Series 1953 F

and over, the Eagle, wild wings outspread, halo of the Stars encircled by puffs of smoke & flame –

a circle the Masonic Pyramid, the sacred Swedenborgian Dollar America, bricked up to the top, & floating surreal above

the triangle of holy outstaring Eye sectioned out of the aire, shining

light emitted from the eyebrowless triangle – and a desert of cactus, scattered all around, clouds afar,

this being the Great Seal of our Passion, Annuit Coeptis, Novus Ordo Seclorum,

the whole surrounded by green spiderwebs designed by T-Men to prevent foul counterfeit –

ONE

S.S. United States, July 1958

'Back on Times Square, Dreaming of Times Square'

Let some sad trumpeter stand
　　　　　on the empty streets at dawn
and blow a silver chorus to the
　　　　　buildings of Times Square,
memorial of ten years, at 5 A.M., with
　　　　　the thin white moon just
　　　　　　　　visible
　　　above the green & grooking McGraw
　　　　　Hill offices
a cop walks by, but he's invisible
　　　　　with his music

The Globe Hotel, Garver lay in
　　　gray beds there and hunched his
　　　back and cleaned his needles –
where I lay many nights on the nod
　　　from his leftover bloody cottons
　　　and dreamed of Blake's voice talking –
　　　　　　I was lonely,
　　　　　　　Garver's dead in Mexico two years,
　　　　hotel's vanished into a parking lot
And I'm back here – sitting on the streets again –
　　　The movies took our language, the
　　　　　great red signs
　　　A DOUBLE BILL OF GASSERS
　　　　　Teen Age Nightmare
　　　Hooligans of the Moon

But we were never nightmare
　　　hooligans but seekers of
　　　　　the blond nose for Truth

Some old men are still alive, but
 the old Junkies are gone –

We are a legend, invisible but
 legendary, as prophesied

New York, July 1958

My Sad Self
   To Frank O'Hara

Sometimes when my eyes are red
I go up on top of the RCA Building
      and gaze at my world, Manhattan –
            my buildings, streets I've done feats in,
               lofts, beds, coldwater flats
– on Fifth Ave below which I also bear in mind,
      its ant cars, little yellow taxis, men
         walking the size of specks of wool –
Panorama of the bridges, sunrise over Brooklyn machine,
      sun go down over New Jersey where I was born
         & Paterson where I played with ants –
my later loves on 15th Street,
      my greater loves of Lower East Side,
         my once fabulous amours in the Bronx
                     faraway –
paths crossing in these hidden streets,
      my history summed up, my absences
         and ecstasies in Harlem –
– sun shining down on all I own
      in one eyeblink to the horizon
         in my last eternity –
                  matter is water.
Sad,
      I take the elevator and go
            down, pondering,
and walk on the pavements staring into all man's
                        plateglass, faces,
         questioning after who loves,
      and stop, bemused
         in front of an automobile shopwindow
      standing lost in calm thought,
         traffic moving up & down 5th Avenue blocks behind me
            waiting for a moment when . . .

Time to go home & cook supper & listen to
                the romantic war news on the radio
                        . . . all movement stops
& I walk in the timeless sadness of existence,
        tenderness flowing thru the buildings,
                my fingertips touching reality's face,
my own face streaked with tears in the mirror
        of some window – at dusk –
                        where I have no desire –
for bonbons – or to own the dresses or Japanese
                lampshades of intellection –

Confused by the spectacle around me,
                Man struggling up the street
                with packages, newspapers,
                                ties, beautiful suits
                toward his desire
        Man, woman, streaming over the pavements
                red lights clocking hurried watches &
                movements at the curb –

And all these streets leading
        so crosswise, honking, lengthily,
                        by avenues
        stalked by high buildings or crusted into slums
                thru such halting traffic
                        screaming cars and engines
so painfully to this
        countryside, this graveyard
                this stillness
                        on deathbed or mountain
        once seen
                never regained or desired
                        in the mind to come
where all Manhattan that I've seen must disappear.

New York, October 1958

Battleship Newsreel

I was high on tea in my fo'c'sle near the forepeak hatch listen-
    ing to the stars
envisioning the kamikazes flapping and turning in the soiled
    clouds
ackack burst into fire a vast hole ripped out of the bow like a
    burning lily
we dumped our oilcans of nitroglycerine among the waving
    octopi
dull thud and boom of thunder undersea the cough of the
    tubercular machinegunner
flames in the hold among the cans of ether the roar of battle-
    ships far away
rolling in the sea like whales surrounded by dying ants the
    screams the captain mad
Suddenly a golden light came over the ocean and grew large the
    radiance entered the sky
a deathly chill and heaviness entered my body I could scarce lift
    my eye
and the ship grew sheathed in light like an overexposed photo-
    graph fading in the brain.

New York, 1959

Kaddish

For Naomi Ginsberg, 1894–1956

I

Strange now to think of you, gone without corsets & eyes, while
I walk on the sunny pavement of Greenwich Village.
downtown Manhattan, clear winter noon, and I've been up all
night, talking, talking, reading the Kaddish aloud, listening
to Ray Charles blues shout blind on the phonograph
the rhythm the rhythm – and your memory in my head three
years after – And read Adonais' last triumphant stanzas
aloud – wept, realizing how we suffer –
And how Death is that remedy all singers dream of, sing,
remember, prophesy as in the Hebrew Anthem, or the
Buddhist Book of Answers – and my own imagination of
a withered leaf – at dawn –
Dreaming back thru life, Your time – and mine accelerating
toward Apocalypse,
the final moment – the flower burning in the Day – and what
comes after,
looking back on the mind itself that saw an American city
a flash away, and the great dream of Me or China, or you
and a phantom Russia, or a crumpled bed that never
existed –
like a poem in the dark – escaped back to Oblivion –
No more to say, and nothing to weep for but the Beings in the
Dream, trapped in its disappearance,
sighing, screaming with it, buying and selling pieces of phantom, worshipping each other,
worshipping the God included in it all – longing or inevitabil-
ity? – while it lasts, a Vision – anything more?
It leaps about me, as I go out and walk the street, look back over
my shoulder, Seventh Avenue, the battlements of window
office buildings shouldering each other high, under a

cloud, tall as the sky an instant – and the sky above – an
old blue place.
or down the Avenue to the south, to – as I walk toward the
Lower East Side – where you walked 50 years ago, little
girl – from Russia, eating the first poisonous tomatoes of
America – frightened on the dock –
then struggling in the crowds of Orchard Street toward what? –
toward Newark –
toward candy store, first home-made sodas of the century,
hand-churned ice cream in backroom on musty brown-
floor boards –
Toward education marriage nervous breakdown, operation,
teaching school, and learning to be mad, in a dream – what
is this life?
Toward the Key in the window – and the great Key lays its head
of light on top of Manhattan, and over the floor, and lays
down on the sidewalk – in a single vast beam, moving, as
I walk down First toward the Yiddish Theater – and the
place of poverty
you knew, and I know, but without caring now – Strange to
have moved thru Paterson, and the West, and Europe and
here again,
with the cries of Spaniards now in the doorstoops doors and
dark boys on the street, fire escapes old as you
– Tho you're not old now, that's left here with me –
Myself, anyhow, maybe as old as the universe – and I guess that
dies with us – enough to cancel all that comes – What
came is gone forever every time –
That's good! That leaves it open for no regret – no fear radia-
tors, lacklove, torture even toothache in the end –
Though while it comes it is a lion that eats the soul – and the
lamb, the soul, in us, alas, offering itself in sacrifice to
change's fierce hunger – hair and teeth – and the roar of
bonepain, skull bare, break rib, rot-skin, braintricked
Implacability.

Ai! ai! we do worse! We are in a fix! And you're out, Death let
     you out, Death had the Mercy, you're done with your cen-
     tury, done with God, done with the path thru it – Done
     with yourself at last – Pure – Back to the Babe dark before
     your Father, before us all – before the world –
There, rest. No more suffering for you. I know where you've
     gone, it's good.
No more flowers in the summer fields of New York, no joy now,
     no more fear of Louis,
and no more of his sweetness and glasses, his high school
     decades, debts, loves, frightened telephone calls, concep-
     tion beds, relatives, hands –
No more of sister Elanor, – she gone before you – we kept it secret
     – you killed her – or she killed herself to bear with you – an
     arthritic heart – But Death's killed you both – No matter –
Nor your memory of your mother, 1915 tears in silent movies
     weeks and weeks – forgetting, agrieve watching Marie
     Dressler address humanity, Chaplin dance in youth,
or Boris Godunov, Chaliapin's at the Met, halling his voice of a
     weeping Czar – by standing room with Elanor & Max –
     watching also the Capitalists take seats in Orchestra, white
     furs, diamonds,
with the YPSL's hitch-hiking thru Pennsylvania, in black baggy
     gym skirts pants, photograph of 4 girls holding each other
     round the waist, and laughing eye, too coy, virginal soli-
     tude of 1920
all girls grown old, or dead, now, and that long hair in the grave
     – lucky to have husbands later –
You made it – I came too – Eugene my brother before (still
     grieving now and will gream on to his last stiff hand, as he
     goes thru his cancer – or kill – later perhaps – soon he will
     think –)
And it's the last moment I remember, which I see them all, thru
     myself, now – tho not you
I didn't foresee what you felt – what more hideous gape of bad
     mouth came first – to you – and were you prepared?

To go where? In that Dark – that – in that God? a radiance? A
   Lord in the Void? Like an eye in the black cloud in a
   dream? Adonoi at last, with you?

Beyond my remembrance! Incapable to guess! Not merely
   the yellow skull in the grave, or a box of worm dust, and
   a stained ribbon – Deaths-head with Halo? can you
   believe it?

Is it only the sun that shines once for the mind, only the flash
   of existence, than none ever was?

Nothing beyond what we have – what you had – that so pitiful
   – yet Triumph,

to have been here, and changed, like a tree, broken, or flower –
   fed to the ground – but mad, with its petals, colored,
   thinking Great Universe, shaken, cut in the head, leaf
   stript, hid in an egg crate hospital, cloth wrapped, sore –
   freaked in the moon brain, Naughtless.

No flower like that flower, which knew itself in the garden, and
   fought the knife – lost

Cut down by an idiot Snowman's icy – even in the Spring –
   strange ghost thought – some Death – Sharp icicle in his
   hand – crowned with old roses – a dog for his eyes – cock
   of a sweatshop – heart of electric irons.

All the accumulations of life, that wear us out – clocks, bodies,
   consciousness, shoes, breasts – begotten sons – your
   Communism – 'Paranoia' into hospitals.

You once kicked Elanor in the leg, she died of heart failure later.
   You of stroke. Asleep? within a year, the two of you, sisters
   in death. Is Elanor happy?

Max grieves alive in an office on Lower Broadway, lone large
   mustache over midnight Accountings, not sure. His life
   passes – as he sees – and what does he doubt now? Still
   dream of making money, or that might have made money,
   hired nurse, had children, found even your Immortality,
   Naomi?

I'll see him soon. Now I've got to cut through – to talk to you –
   as I didn't when you had a mouth.

Forever. And we're bound for that, Forever – like Emily
    Dickinson's horses – headed to the End.
They know the way – These Steeds – run faster than we think –
    it's our own life they cross – and take with them.

Magnificent, mourned no more, marred of heart, mind
behind, married dreamed, mortal changed – Ass and face done
with murder.
    In the world, given, flower maddened, made no Utopia,
shut under pine, almed in Earth, balmed in Lone, Jehovah,
accept.
    Nameless, One Faced, Forever beyond me, beginningless,
endless, Father in death. Tho I am not there for this Prophecy,
I am unmarried, I'm hymnless, I'm Heavenless, headless in
blisshood I would still adore
    Thee, Heaven, after Death, only One blessed in
Nothingness, not light or darkness, Dayless Eternity –
    Take this, this Psalm, from me, burst from my hand in a
day, some of my Time, now given to Nothing – to praise Thee
– But Death
    This is the end, the redemption from Wilderness, way for
the Wonderer, House sought for All, black handkerchief washed
clean by weeping – page beyond Psalm – Last change of mine
and Naomi – to God's perfect Darkness – Death, stay thy phantoms!

II

    Over and over – refrain – of the Hospitals – still haven't
written your history – leave it abstract – a few images
    run thru the mind – like the saxophone chorus of houses
and years – remembrance of electrical shocks.
    By long nites as a child in Paterson apartment, watching
over your nervousness – you were fat – your next move –
    By that afternoon I stayed home from school to take
care of you – once and for all – when I vowed forever that once
man disagreed with my opinion of the cosmos, I was lost –

64

By my later burden – vow to illuminate mankind – this is release of particulars – (mad as you) – (sanity a trick of agreement) –

But you stared out the window on the Broadway Church corner, and spied a mystical assassin from Newark,

So phoned the Doctor – 'OK go way for a rest' – so I put on my coat and walked you downstreet – On the way a grammar-school boy screamed, unaccountably – 'Where you goin Lady to Death'? I shuddered –

and you covered your nose with motheaten fur collar, gas mask against poison sneaked into downtown atmosphere, sprayed by Grandma –

And was the driver of the cheesebox Public Service bus a member of the gang? You shuddered at his face, I could hardly get you on – to New York, very Times Square, to grab another Greyhound –

where we hung around 2 hours fighting invisible bugs and jewish sickness – breeze poisoned by Roosevelt –

out to get you – and me tagging along, hoping it would end in a quiet room in a Victorian house by a lake.

Ride 3 hours thru tunnels past all American industry, Bayonne preparing for World War II, tanks, gas fields, soda factories, diners, locomotive roundhouse fortress – into piney woods New Jersey Indians – calm towns – long roads thru sandy tree fields –

Bridges by deerless creeks, old wampum loading the streambed – down there a tomahawk or Pocahontas bone – and a million old ladies voting for Roosevelt in brown small houses, roads off the Madness highway –

perhaps a hawk in a tree, or a hermit looking for an owl-filled branch –

All the time arguing – afraid of strangers in the forward double seat, snoring regardless – what busride they snore on now?

'Allen, you don't understand – it's – ever since those 3 big sticks up my back – they did something to me in Hospital, they poisoned me, they want to see me dead – 3 big sticks, 3 big sticks –

'The Bitch! Old Grandma! Last week I saw her, dressed in pants like an old man, with a sack on her back, climbing up the brick side of the apartment

'On the fire escape, with poison germs, to throw on me – at night – maybe Louis is helping her – he's under her power –

'I'm your mother, take me to Lakewood' (near where Graf Zeppelin had crashed before, all Hitler in Explosion) 'where I can hide.'

We got there – Dr. Whatzis rest home – she hid behind a closet – demanded a blood transfusion.

We were kicked out – tramping with Valise to unknown shady lawn houses – dusk, pine trees after dark – long dead street filled with crickets and poison ivy –

I shut her up by now – big house REST HOME ROOMS – gave the landlady her money for the week – carried up the iron valise – sat on bed waiting to escape –

Neat room in attic with friendly bedcover – lace curtains – spinning wheel rug – Stained wallpaper old as Naomi. We were home.

I left on the next bus to New York – laid my head back in the last seat, depressed – the worst yet to come? – abandoning her, rode in torpor – I was only 12.

Would she hide in her room and come out cheerful for breakfast? Or lock her door and stare thru the window for side-street spies? Listen at keyholes for Hitlerian invisible gas? Dream in a chair – or mock me, by – in front of a mirror, alone?

12 riding the bus at nite thru New Jersey, have left Naomi to Parcae in Lakewood's haunted house – left to my own fate bus – sunk in a seat – all violins broken – my heart sore in my ribs – mind was empty – Would she were safe in her coffin –

Or back at Normal School in Newark, studying up on America in a black skirt – winter on the street without lunch – a penny a pickle – home at night to take care of Elanor in the bedroom –

First nervous breakdown was 1919 – she stayed home from school and lay in a dark room for three weeks – something bad – never said what – every noise hurt – dreams of the creaks of Wall Street –

Before the gray Depression – went upstate New York – recovered – Lou took photo of her sitting crossleg on the grass – her long hair wound with flowers – smiling – playing lullabies on mandolin – poison ivy smoke in left-wing summer camps and me in infancy saw trees –

or back teaching school, laughing with idiots, the backward classes – her Russian specialty – morons with dreamy lips, great eyes, thin feet & sicky fingers, swaybacked, rachitic –

great heads pendulous over Alice in Wonderland, a blackboard full of C A T.

Naomi reading patiently, story out of a Communist fairy book – Tale of the Sudden Sweetness of the Dictator – Forgiveness of Warlocks – Armies Kissing –

Deathsheads Around the Green Table – The King & the Workers – Paterson Press printed them up in the '30s till she went mad, or they folded, both.

O Paterson! I got home late that nite. Louis was worried. How could I be so – didn't I think? I shouldn't have left her. Mad in Lakewood. Call the Doctor. Phone the home in the pines. Too late.

Went to bed exhausted, wanting to leave the world (probably that year newly in love with R – my high school mind hero, jewish boy who came a doctor later – then silent neat kid –

I later laying down life for him, moved to Manhattan – followed him to college – Prayed on ferry to help mankind if admitted – vowed, the day I journeyed to Entrance Exam –

by being honest revolutionary labor lawyer – would train for that – inspired by Sacco Vanzetti, Norman Thomas, Debs, Altgeld, Sandburg, Poe – Little Blue Books. I wanted to be President, or Senator.

ignorant woe – later dreams of kneeling by R's shocked knees declaring my love of 1941 – What sweetness he'd have shown me, tho, that I'd wished him & despaired – first love – a crush –

Later a mortal avalanche, whole mountains of homosexuality, Matterhorns of cock, Grand Canyons of asshole – weight on my melancholy head –

meanwhile I walked on Broadway imagining Infinity like a rubber ball without space beyond – what's outside? – coming home to Graham Avenue still melancholy passing the lone green hedges across the street, dreaming after the movies –)

The telephone rang at 2 A.M. – Emergency – she'd gone mad – Naomi hiding under the bed screaming bugs of Mussolini – Help! Louis! Buba! Fascists! Death! – the landlady frightened – old fag attendant screaming back at her –

Terror, that woke the neighbors – old ladies on the second floor recovering from menopause – all those rags between thighs, clean sheets, sorry over lost babies – husbands ashen – children sneering at Yale, or putting oil in hair at CCNY – or trembling in Montclair State Teachers College like Eugene –

Her big leg crouched to her breast, hand outstretched Keep Away, wool dress on her thighs, fur coat dragged under the bed – she barricaded herself under bedspring with suitcases.

Louis in pajamas listening to phone, frightened – do now? – Who could know? – my fault, delivering her to solitude? – sitting in the dark room on the sofa, trembling, to figure out –

He took the morning train to Lakewood, Naomi still under bed – thought he brought poison Cops – Naomi screaming – Louis what happened to your heart then? Have you been killed by Naomi's ecstasy?

Dragged her out, around the corner, a cab, forced her in with valise, but the driver left them off at drugstore. Bus stop, two hours' wait.

I lay in bed nervous in the 4-room apartment, the big bed in living room, next to Louis' desk – shaking – he came home that nite, late, told me what happened.

Naomi at the prescription counter defending herself from the enemy – racks of children's books, douche bags, aspirins, posts, blood – 'Don't come near me – murderers! Keep away! Promise not to kill me!'

Louis in horror at the soda fountain – with Lakewood girlscouts – Coke addicts – nurses – busmen hung on schedule – Police from country precinct, dumbed – and a priest dreaming of pigs on an ancient cliff?

Smelling the air – Louis pointing to emptiness? – Customers vomiting their Cokes – or staring – Louis humiliated – Naomi triumphant – The Announcement of the Plot. Bus arrives, the drivers won't have them on trip to New York.

Phonecalls to Dr. Whatzis, 'She needs a rest,' The mental hospital – State Greystone Doctors – 'Bring her here, Mr. Ginsberg.'

Naomi, Naomi – sweating, bulge-eyed, fat, the dress unbuttoned at one side – hair over brow, her stocking hanging evilly on her legs – screaming for a blood transfusion – one righteous hand upraised – a shoe in it – barefoot in the Pharmacy –

The enemies approach – what poisons? Tape recorders? FBI? Zhdanov hiding behind the counter? Trotsky mixing rat bacteria in the back of the store? Uncle Sam in Newark, plotting deathly perfumes in the Negro district? Uncle Ephraim, drunk with murder in the politician's bar, scheming of Hague? Aunt Rose passing water thru the needles of the Spanish Civil War?

till the hired $35 ambulance came from Red Bank—Grabbed her arms – strapped her on the stretcher – moaning, poisoned by imaginaries, vomiting chemicals thru Jersey, begging mercy from Essex County to Morristown –

And back to Greystone where she lay three years – that was the last breakthrough, delivered her to Madhouse again –

On what wards – I walked there later, oft – old catatonic ladies, gray as cloud or ash or walls – sit crooning over floorspace – Chairs – and the wrinkled hags acreep, accusing – begging my 13-year-old mercy –

'Take me home' – I went alone sometimes looking for the lost Naomi, taking Shock – and I'd say, 'No, you're crazy Mama, – Trust the Drs.' –

And Eugene, my brother, her elder son, away studying Law in a furnished room in Newark –

came Paterson-ward next day – and he sat on the broken-down couch in the living room – 'We had to send her back to Greystone' –

– his face perplexed, so young, then eyes with tears – then crept weeping all over his face – 'What for?' wail vibrating in his cheekbones, eyes closed up, high voice – Eugene's face of pain.

Him faraway, escaped to an Elevator in the Newark Library, his bottle daily milk on windowsill of $5 week furn room downtown at trolley tracks –

He worked 8 hrs. a day for $20/wk – thru Law School years – stayed by himself innocent near negro whore-houses.

Unlaid, poor virgin – writing poems about Ideals and politics letters to the editor Pat Eve News – (we both wrote, denouncing Senator Borah and Isolationists – and felt mysterious toward Paterson City Hall –

I sneaked inside it once – local Moloch tower with phallus spire & cap o' ornament, strange gothic Poetry that stood on Market Street – replica Lyons' Hotel de Ville –

wings, balcony & scrollwork portals, gateway to the giant city clock, secret map room full of Hawthorne – dark Debs in the Board of Tax – Rembrandt smoking in the gloom –

Silent polished desks in the great committee room – Aldermen? Bd of Finance? Mosca the hairdresser aplot – Crapp the gangster issuing orders from the john – The madmen struggling over Zone, Fire, Cops & Backroom Metaphysics – we're all dead – outside by the bus stop Eugene stared thru childhood –

where the Evangelist preached madly for 3 decades, hard-haired, cracked & true to his mean Bible – chalked Prepare to Meet Thy God on civic pave –

or God is Love on the railroad overpass concrete – he raved like I would rave, the lone Evangelist – Death on City Hall –)

But Gene, young, – been Montclair Teachers College 4 years – taught half year & quit to go ahead in life – afraid of Discipline Problems – dark sex Italian students, raw girls getting laid, no English, sonnets disregarded – and he did not know much – just that he lost –

so broke his life in two and paid for Law – read huge blue books and rode the ancient elevator 13 miles away in Newark & studied up hard for the future

just found the Scream of Naomi on his failure doorstep, for the final time, Naomi gone, us lonely – home – him sitting there –

Then have some chicken soup, Eugene. The Man of Evangel wails in front of City Hall. And this year Lou has poetic loves of suburb middle age – in secret – music from his 1937 book – Sincere – he longs for beauty –

No love since Naomi screamed – since 1923? – now lost in Greystone ward – new shock for her – Electricity, following the 40 Insulin.

And Metrazol had made her fat.

So that a few years later she came home again – we'd much advanced and planned – I waited for that day – my Mother again to cook & – play the piano – sing at mandolin – Lung Stew, & Stenka Razin, & the communist line on the war with Finland – and Louis in debt – suspected to be poisoned money – mysterious capitalisms

– & walked down the long front hall & looked at the furniture. She never remembered it all. Some amnesia. Examined the doilies – and the dining room set was sold –

the Mahogany table – 20 years love – gone to the junk man – we still had the piano – and the book of Poe – and the Mandolin, tho needed some string, dusty –

She went to the backroom to lie down in bed and ruminate, or nap, hide – I went in with her, not leave her by herself – lay in bed next to her – shades pulled, dusky, late afternoon – Louis in front room at desk, waiting – perhaps boiling chicken for supper –

'Don't be afraid of me because I'm just coming back home from the mental hospital – I'm your mother –'

Poor love, lost – a fear – I lay there – Said, 'I love you Naomi,' – stiff, next to her arm. I would have cried, was this the comfortless lone union? – Nervous, and she got up soon.

Was she ever satisfied? And – by herself sat on the new couch by the front windows, uneasy – cheek leaning on her hand – narrowing eye – at what fate that day –

Picking her tooth with her nail, lips formed an O, suspicion – thought's old worn vagina – absent sideglance of eye – some evil debt written in the wall, unpaid – & the aged breasts of Newark come near –

May have heard radio gossip thru the wires in her head, controlled by 3 big sticks left in her back by gangsters in amnesia, thru the hospital – caused pain between her shoulders –

Into her head – Roosevelt should know her case, she told me – Afraid to kill her, now, that the government knew their names – traced back to Hitler – wanted to leave Louis' house forever.

One night, sudden attack – her noise in the bathroom – like croaking up her soul – convulsions and red vomit coming out of her mouth – diarrhea water exploding from her behind – on all fours in front of the toilet – urine running between her legs – left retching on the tile floor smeared with her black feces – unfainted –

At forty, varicosed, nude, fat, doomed, hiding outside the apartment door near the elevator calling Police, yelling for her girlfriend Rose to help –

Once locked herself in with razor or iodine – could hear her cough in tears at sink – Lou broke through glass green-painted door, we pulled her out to the bedroom.

Then quiet for months that winter – walks, alone, nearby on Broadway, read Daily Worker – Broke her arm, fell on icy street –

Began to scheme escape from cosmic financial murder plots – later she ran away to the Bronx to her sister Elanor. And there's another saga of late Naomi in New York.

Or thru Elanor or the Workmen's Circle, where she worked, addressing envelopes, she made out – went shopping for Campbell's tomato soup – saved money Louis mailed her –

Later she found a boyfriend, and he was a doctor – Dr. Isaac worked for National Maritime Union – now Italian bald and pudgy old doll – who was himself an orphan – but they kicked him out – Old cruelties –

Sloppier, sat around on bed or chair, in corset dreaming to herself – 'I'm hot – I'm getting fat – I used to have such a beautiful figure before I went to the hospital – You should have seen me in Woodbine –' This in a furnished room around the NMU hall, 1943.

Looking at naked baby pictures in the magazine – baby powder advertisements, strained lamb carrots – 'I will think nothing but beautiful thoughts.'

Revolving her head round and round on her neck at window light in summertime, in hypnotize, in doven-dream recall –

'I touch his cheek, I touch his cheek, he touches my lips with his hand, I think beautiful thoughts, the baby has a beautiful hand.' –

Or a No-shake of her body, disgust – some thought of Buchenwald – some insulin passes thru her head – a grimace nerve shudder at Involuntary (as shudder when I piss) – bad chemical in her cortex – 'No don't think of that. He's a rat.'

Naomi: 'And when we die we become an onion, a cabbage, a carrot, or a squash, a vegetable.' I come downtown from Columbia and agree. She reads the Bible, thinks beautiful thoughts all day.

'Yesterday I saw God. What did he look like? Well, in the afternoon I climbed up a ladder – he has a cheap cabin in the country, like Monroe, N.Y. the chicken farms in the wood. He was a lonely old man with a white beard.

'I cooked supper for him. I made him a nice supper – lentil soup, vegetables, bread & butter – miltz – he sat down at the table and ate, he was sad.

'I told him, Look at all those fightings and killings down there, What's the matter? Why don't you put a stop to it?

'I try, he said – That's all he could do, he looked tired. He's a bachelor so long, and he likes lentil soup.'

Serving me meanwhile, a plate of cold fish – chopped raw cabbage dript with tapwater – smelly tomatoes – week-old health food – grated beets & carrots with leaky juice, warm – more and more disconsolate food – I can't eat it for nausea sometimes – the Charity of her hands stinking with Manhattan, madness, desire to please me, cold undercooked fish – pale red near the bones. Her smells – and oft naked in the room, so that I stare ahead, or turn a book ignoring her.

One time I thought she was trying to make me come lay her – flirting to herself at sink – lay back on huge bed that filled most of the room, dress up round her hips, big slash of hair, scars of operations, pancreas, belly wounds, abortions, appendix, stitching of incisions pulling down in the fat like hideous thick zippers – ragged long lips between her legs – What, even, smell of asshole? I was cold – later revolted a little, not much – seemed perhaps a good idea to try – know the Monster of the Beginning Womb – Perhaps – that way. Would she care? She needs a lover.

Yisborach, v'yistabach, v'yispoar, v'yisroman, v'yisnaseh, v'yishador, v'yishalleh, v'yishallol, sh'meh d'kudsho, b'rich hu.

And Louis reestablishing himself in Paterson grimy apartment in negro district – living in dark rooms – but found himself a girl he later married, falling in love again – tho sere & shy – hurt with 20 years Naomi's mad idealism.

Once I came home, after longtime in N.Y., he's lonely – sitting in the bedroom, he at desk chair turned round to face me – weeps, tears in red eyes under his glasses –

That we'd left him – Gene gone strangely into army – she out on her own in N.Y., almost childish in her furnished room. So Louis walked down-town to postoffice to get mail, taught in highschool – stayed at poetry desk, forlorn – ate grief at Bickford's all these years – are gone.

Eugene got out of the Army, came home changed and lone – cut off his nose in jewish operation – for years stopped girls on Broadway for cups of coffee to get laid – Went to NYU, serious there, to finish Law. –

And Gene lived with her, ate naked fishcakes, cheap, while she got crazier – He got thin, or felt helpless, Naomi striking 1920 poses at the moon, half-naked in the next bed.

bit his nails and studied – was the weird nurse-son – Next year he moved to a room near Columbia – though she wanted to live with her children –

'Listen to your mother's plea, I beg you' – Louis still sending her checks – I was in bughouse that year 8 months – my own visions unmentioned in this here Lament –

But then went half mad – Hitler in her room, she saw his mustache in the sink – afraid of Dr. Isaac now, suspecting that he was in on the Newark plot – went up to Bronx to live near Elanor's Rheumatic Heart –

And Uncle Max never got up before noon, tho Naomi at 6 A.M. was listening to the radio for spies – or searching the windowsill,

for in the empty lot downstairs, an old man creeps with his bag stuffing packages of garbage in his hanging black overcoat.

Max's sister Edie works – 17 years bookkeeper at Gimbels – lived downstairs in apartment house, divorced – so Edie took in Naomi on Rochambeau Ave –

Woodlawn Cemetery across the street, vast dale of graves where Poe once – Last stop on Bronx subway – lots of communists in that area.

Who enrolled for painting classes at night in Bronx Adult High School – walked alone under Van Cortlandt Elevated line to class – paints Naomiisms –

Humans sitting on the grass in some Camp No-Worry summers yore – saints with droopy faces and long-ill-fitting pants, from hospital –

Brides in front of Lower East Side with short grooms – lost El trains running over the Babylonian apartment rooftops in the Bronx –

Sad paintings – but she expressed herself. Her mandolin gone, all strings broke in her head, she tried. Toward Beauty? or some old life Message?

But started kicking Elanor, and Elanor had heart trouble – came upstairs and asked her about Spydom for hours, – Elanor frazzled. Max away at office, accounting for cigar stores till at night.

'I am a great woman – am truly a beautiful soul – and because of that they (Hitler, Grandma, Hearst, the Capitalists, Franco, Daily News, the '20s, Mussolini, the living dead) want to shut me up – Buba's the head of a spider network –'

Kicking the girls, Edie & Elanor – Woke Edie at midnite to tell her she was a spy and Elanor a rat. Edie worked all day and couldn't take it – She was organizing the union. – And Elanor began dying, upstairs in bed.

The relatives call me up, she's getting worse – I was the only one left – Went on the subway with Eugene to see her, ate stale fish –

'My sister whispers in the radio – Louis must be in the apartment – his mother tells him what to say – LIARS! – I cooked for my two children – I played the mandolin –'

Last night the nightingale woke me / Last night when all was still / it sang in the golden moonlight / from on the wintry hill. She did.

I pushed her against the door and shouted 'DON'T KICK ELANOR!' – she stared at me – Contempt – die – disbelief her sons are so naive, so dumb – 'Elanor is the worst spy! She's taking orders!'

'– No wires in the room!' – I'm yelling at her – last ditch, Eugene listening on the bed – what can he do to escape that fatal Mama – 'You've been away from Louis years already – Grandma's too old to walk –'

We're all alive at once then – even me & Gene & Naomi in one mythological Cousinesque room – screaming at each other in the Forever – I in Columbia jacket, she half undressed.

I banging against her head which saw Radios, Sticks, Hitlers – the gamut of Hallucinations – for real – her own universe – no road that goes elsewhere – to my own – No America, not even a world –

That you go as all men, as Van Gogh, as mad Hannah, all the same – to the last doom – Thunder, Spirits, Lightning!

I've seen your grave! O strange Naomi! My own – cracked grave! Shema Y'Israel – I am Svul Avrum – you – in death?

Your last night in the darkness of the Bronx – I phonecalled – thru hospital to secret police

that came, when you and I were alone, shrieking at Elanor in my ear – who breathed hard in her own bed, got thin –

Nor will forget, the doorknock, at your fright of spies, – Law advancing, on my honor – Eternity entering the room – you running to the bathroom undressed, hiding in protest from the last heroic fate – staring at my eyes, betrayed – the final cops of madness rescuing me – from your foot against the broken heart of Elanor,

your voice at Edie weary of Gimbels coming home to broken radio – and Louis needing a poor divorce, he wants to get married soon – Eugene dreaming, hiding at 125 St.,

suing negroes for money on crud furniture, defending black
girls –

Protests from the bathroom – Said you were sane – dress-
ing in a cotton robe, your shoes, then new, your purse and
newspaper clippings – no – your honesty –

as you vainly made your lips more real with lipstick, looking in the mirror to see if the Insanity was Me or a carful of
police.

or Grandma spying at 78 – Your vision – Her climbing over
the walls of the cemetery with political kidnapper's bag – or
what you saw on the walls of the Bronx, in pink nightgown at
midnight, staring out the window on the empty lot –

Ah Rochambeau Ave. – Playground of Phantoms –
last apartment in the Bronx for spies – last home for Elanor or
Naomi, here these communist sisters lost their revolution –

'All right – put on your coat Mrs. – let's go – We have
the wagon downstairs – you want to come with her to the
station?'

The ride then – held Naomi's hand, and held her head to
my breast, I'm taller – kissed her and said I did it for the best –
Elanor sick – and Max with heart condition – Needs –

To me – 'Why did you do this?' – 'Yes Mrs., your son will
have to leave you in an hour' – The Ambulance

came in a few hours – drove off at 4 A.M. to some Bellevue
in the night downtown – gone to the hospital forever. I saw her
led away – she waved, tears in her eyes.

Two years, after a trip to Mexico – bleak in the flat plain
near Brent-wood, scrub brush and grass around the unused RR
train track to the crazyhouse –

new brick 20 story central building – lost on the vast lawns
of mad-town on Long Island – huge cities of the moon.

Asylum spreads out giant wings above the path to a
minute black hole – the door – entrance thru crotch –

I went in – smelt funny – the halls again – up elevator – to
a glass door on a Women's Ward – to Naomi – Two nurses

buxom white – They led her out, Naomi stared – and I gaspt – She'd had a stroke –

Too thin, shrunk on her bones – age come to Naomi – now broken into white hair – loose dress on her skeleton – face sunk, old! withered – cheek of crone –

One hand stiff – heaviness of forties & menopause reduced by one heart stroke, lame now – wrinkles – a scar on her head, the lobotomy – ruin, the hand dipping downwards to death –

O Russian faced, woman on the grass, your long black hair is crowned with flowers, the mandolin is on your knees –

Communist beauty, sit here married in the summer among daisies, promised happiness at hand –

holy mother, now you smile on your love, your world is born anew, children run naked in the field spotted with dandelions,

they eat in the plum tree grove at the end of the meadow and find a cabin where a white-haired negro teaches the mystery of his rainbarrel –

blessed daughter come to America, I long to hear your voice again, remembering your mother's music, in the Song of the Natural Front –

O glorious muse that bore me from the womb, gave suck first mystic life & taught me talk and music, from whose pained head I first took Vision –

Tortured and beaten in the skull – What mad hallucinations of the damned that drive me out of my own skull to seek Eternity till I find Peace for Thee, O Poetry – and for all humankind call on the Origin

Death which is the mother of the universe! – Now wear your nakedness forever, white flowers in your hair, your marriage sealed behind the sky – no revolution might destroy that maidenhood –

O beautiful Garbo of my Karma – all photographs from 1920 in Camp Nicht-Gedeiget here unchanged – with all the teachers from Newark – Nor Elanor be gone, nor Max await his specter – nor Louis retire from this High School –

Back! You! Naomi! Skull on you! Gaunt immortality and revolution come – small broken woman – the ashen indoor eyes of hospitals, ward grayness on skin –

'Are you a spy?' I sat at the sour table, eyes filling with tears – 'Who are you? Did Louis send you? – The wires –'

in her hair, as she beat on her head – 'I'm not a bad girl – don't murder me! – I hear the ceiling – I raised two children –'

Two years since I'd been there – I started to cry – She stared – nurse broke up the meeting a moment – I went into the bathroom to hide, against the toilet white walls

'The Horror' I weeping – to see her again – 'The Horror' – as if she were dead thru funeral rot in – 'The Horror!'

I came back she yelled more – they led her away – 'You're not Allen –' I watched her face – but she passed by me, not looking –

Opened the door to the ward, – she went thru without a glance back, quiet suddenly – I stared out – she looked old – the verge of the grave – 'All the Horror!'

Another year, I left N.Y. – on West Coast in Berkeley cottage dreamed of her soul – that, thru life, in what form it stood in that body, ashen or manic, gone beyond joy –

near its death – with eyes – was my own love in its form, the Naomi, my mother on earth still – sent her long letter – & wrote hymns to the mad – Work of the merciful Lord of Poetry.

that causes the broken grass to be green, or the rock to break in grass – or the Sun to be constant to earth – Sun of all sunflowers and days on bright iron bridges – what shines on old hospitals – as on my yard –

Returning from San Francisco one night, Orlovsky in my room – Whalen in his peaceful chair – a telegram from Gene, Naomi dead –

Outside I bent my head to the ground under the bushes near the garage – knew she was better –

at last – not left to look on Earth alone – 2 years of solitude – no one, at age nearing 60 – old woman of skulls – once long-tressed Naomi of Bible –

or Ruth who wept in America – Rebecca aged in Newark – David remembering his Harp, now lawyer at Yale

or Svul Avrum – Israel Abraham – myself – to sing in the wilderness toward God – O Elohim! – so to the end – 2 days after her death I got her letter –

Strange Prophecies anew! She wrote – 'The key is in the window, the key is in the sunlight at the window – I have the key – Get married Allen don't take drugs – the key is in the bars, in the sunlight in the window.

> Love,
>> your mother'

which is Naomi –

Hymmnn

In the world which He has created according to his will Blessed
  Praised

Magnified Lauded Exalted the Name of the Holy One Blessed
  is He!

In the house in Newark Blessed is He! In the madhouse Blessed
  is He! In the house of Death Blessed is He!

Blessed be He in homosexuality! Blessed be He in Paranoia!
  Blessed be He in the city! Blessed be He in the Book!

Blessed be He who dwells in the shadow! Blessed be He! Blessed
  be He!

Blessed be you Naomi in tears! Blessed be you Naomi in fears!
  Blessed Blessed Blessed in sickness!

Blessed be you Naomi in Hospitals! Blessed be you Naomi in
  solitude! Blest be your triumph! Blest be your bars! Blest
  be your last years' loneliness!

Blest be your failure! Blest be your stroke! Blest be the close of
your eye!
Blest be the gaunt of your cheek! Blest be your withered thighs!
Blessed be Thee Naomi in Death! Blessed be Death! Blessed be
Death!
Blessed be He Who leads all sorrow to Heaven! Blessed be He
in the end!
Blessed be He who builds Heaven in Darkness! Blessed Blessed
Blessed be He! Blessed be He! Blessed be Death on us All!

III

Only to have not forgotten the beginning in which she drank
cheap sodas in the morgues of Newark,
only to have seen her weeping on gray tables in long wards of
her universe
only to have known the weird ideas of Hitler at the door, the
wires in her head, the three big sticks
rammed down her back, the voices in the ceiling shrieking out
her ugly early lays for 30 years,
only to have seen the time-jumps, memory lapse, the crash of
wars, the roar and silence of a vast electric shock,
only to have seen her painting crude pictures of Elevateds
running over the rooftops of the Bronx
her brothers dead in Riverside or Russia, her lone in Long
Island writing a last letter – and her image in the sunlight
at the window
'The key is in the sunlight at the window in the bars the key is
in the sunlight,'
only to have come to that dark night on iron bed by stroke when
the sun gone down on Long Island
and the vast Atlantic roars outside the great call of Being to its
own
to come back out of the Nightmare – divided creation – with
her head lain on a pillow of the hospital to die
– in one last glimpse – all Earth one everlasting Light in the
familiar black-out – no tears for this vision –

But that the key should be left behind – at the window – the key
    in the sunlight – to the living – that can take
that slice of light in hand – and turn the door – and look
    back see
Creation glistening backwards to the same grave, size of universe,
size of the tick of the hospital's clock on the archway over the
    white door –

IV

O mother
what have I left out
O mother
what have I forgotten
O mother
farewell
with a long black shoe
farewell
with Communist Party and a broken stocking
farewell
with six dark hairs on the wen of your breast
farewell
with your old dress and a long black beard around the vagina
farewell
with your sagging belly
with your fear of Hitler
with your mouth of bad short stories
with your fingers of rotten mandolins
with your arms of fat Paterson porches
with your belly of strikes and smokestacks
with your chin of Trotsky and the Spanish War
with your voice singing for the decaying overbroken workers
with your nose of bad lay with your nose of the smell of the
    pickles of Newark
with your eyes
with your eyes of Russia

with your eyes of no money
with your eyes of false China
with your eyes of Aunt Elanor
with your eyes of starving India
with your eyes pissing in the park
with your eyes of America taking a fall
with your eyes of your failure at the piano
with your eyes of your relatives in California
with your eyes of Ma Rainey dying in an aumbulance
with your eyes of Czechoslovakia attacked by robots
with your eyes going to painting class at night in the Bronx
with your eyes of the killer Grandma you see on the horizon
        from the Fire-Escape
with your eyes running naked out of the apartment screaming
        into the hall
with your eyes being led away by policemen to an ambulance
with your eyes strapped down on the operating table
with your eyes with the pancreas removed
with your eyes of appendix operation
with your eyes of abortion
with your eyes of ovaries removed
with your eyes of shock
with your eyes of lobotomy
with your eyes of divorce
with your eyes of stroke
with your eyes alone
with your eyes
with your eyes
with your Death full of Flowers

                V

Caw caw caw crows shriek in the white sun over grave stones in
        Long Island
Lord Lord Lord Naomi underneath this grass my halflife and
        my own as hers

caw caw my eye be buried in the same Ground where I stand in
    Angel

Lord Lord great Eye that stares on All and moves in a black
    cloud

caw caw strange cry of Beings flung up into sky over the waving
    trees

Lord Lord O Grinder of giant Beyonds my voice in a boundless
    field in Sheol

Caw caw the call of Time rent out of foot and wing an instant
    in the universe

Lord Lord an echo in the sky the wind through ragged leaves
    the roar of memory

caw caw all years my birth a dream caw caw New York the bus
    the broken shoe the vast highschool caw caw all Visions of
    the Lord

Lord Lord Lord caw caw caw Lord Lord Lord caw caw caw Lord

Paris, December 1957–New York, 1959

Psalm IV

Now I'll record my secret vision, impossible sight of the face of
     God:

It was no dream, I lay broad waking on a fabulous couch in
     Harlem

having masturbated for no love, and read half naked an open
     book of Blake on my lap

Lo & behold! I was thoughtless and turned a page and gazed on
     the living Sun-flower

and heard a voice, it was Blake's, reciting in earthen measure:

the voice rose out of the page to my secret ear never heard
     before –

I lifted my eyes to the window, red walls of buildings flashed
     outside, endless sky sad in Eternity

sunlight gazing on the world, apartments of Harlem standing
     in the universe –

each brick and cornice stained with intelligence like a vast
     living face –

the great brain unfolding and brooding in wilderness! – Now
     speaking aloud with Blake's voice –

Love! thou patient presence & bone of the body! Father! thy
     careful watching and waiting over my soul!

My son! My son! the endless ages have remembered me! My
     son! My son! Time howled in anguish in my ear!

My son! My son! my father wept and held me in his dead arms.

1960

To P.O.

The whitewashed room, roof
of a third-rate Mohammedan hotel,
two beds, blurred fan
whirling over yr brown guitar,
knapsack open on floor, towel
hanging from chair, Orange Crush,
brown paper manuscript packages,
Tibetan tankas, Gandhi pajamas,
Ramakrishna *Gospel*, bright umbrella
a mess on a rickety wooden stand,
the yellow wall-bulb lights up
this scene Calcutta for the thirtieth night –
Come in the green door, long Western gold
hair plastered down your shoulders
from shower: 'Did we take our pills
this week for malaria?' Happy birthday
dear Peter, your 29th year.

Calcutta, July 8, 1962

I Am a Victim of Telephone

When I lie down to sleep dream the Wishing Well it
    rings
'Have you a new play for the brokendown theater?'
When I write in my notebook poem it rings
'Buster Keaton is under the brooklyn bridge on Frankfurt and
    Pearl . . .'
When I unsheath my skin extend my cock toward someone's
    thighs fat or thin, boy or girl
Tingaling – 'Please get him out of jail . . . the police are crashing
    down.'
When I lift the soupspoon to my lips, the phone on the floor
    begins purring
'Hello it's me – I'm in the park two broads from Iowa
    . . . nowhere to sleep last night . . . hit 'em in the mouth'
When I muse at smoke crawling over the roof outside my street
    window
purifying Eternity with my eye observation of gray vaporous
    columns in the sky
ring ring 'Hello this is Esquire be a dear and finish your political
    commitment manifesto'
When I listen to radio presidents roaring on the convention
    floor
the phone also chimes in 'Rush up to Harlem with us and see
    the riots'
Always the telephone linked to all the hearts of the world
    beating at once
crying my husband's gone my boyfriend's busted forever my
    poetry was rejected
won't you come over for money and please won't you write me
    a piece of bullshit
How are you dear can you come to Easthampton we're all here
    bathing in the ocean we're all so lonely

and I lie back on my pallet contemplating $50 phone bill, broke, drowsy, anxious, my heart fearful of the fingers dialing, the deaths, the singing of telephone bells
ringing at dawn ringing all afternoon ringing up midnight ringing now forever.

New York, June 20, 1964

Kral Majales

And the Communists have nothing to offer but fat cheeks and
    eyeglasses and lying policemen
and the Capitalists proffer Napalm and money in green suit-
    cases to the Naked,
and the Communists create heavy industry but the heart is also
    heavy
and the beautiful engineers are all dead, the secret technicians
    conspire for their own glamour
in the Future, in the Future, but now drink vodka and lament
    the Security Forces,
and the Capitalists drink gin and whiskey on airplanes but let
    Indian brown millions starve
and when Communist and Capitalist assholes tangle the Just
    man is arrested or robbed or had his head cut off,
but not like Kabir, and the cigarette cough of the Just man above
    the clouds
in the bright sunshine is a salute to the health of the blue sky.
For I was arrested thrice in Prague, once for singing drunk on
    Narodni street,
once knocked down on the midnight pavement by a mustached
    agent who screamed out BOUZERANT,
once for losing my notebooks of unusual sex politics dream
    opinions,
and I was sent from Havana by plane by detectives in green
    uniform,
and I was sent from Prague by plane by detectives in
    Czechoslovakian business suits,
Cardplayers out of Cézanne, the two strange dolls that entered
    Joseph K's room at morn
also entered mine, and ate at my table, and examined my scrib-
    bles,
and followed me night and morn from the houses of lovers to
    the cafés of Centrum –

And I am the King of May, which is the power of sexual
youth,

and I am the King of May, which is industry in eloquence and
action in amour,

and I am the King of May, which is long hair of Adam and the
Beard of my own body

and I am the King of May, which is Kral Majales in the
Czechoslovakian tongue,

and I am the King of May, which is old Human poesy, and
100,000 people chose my name,

and I am the King of May, and in a few minutes I will land at
London Airport,

and I am the King of May, naturally, for I am of Slavic parent-
age and a Buddhist Jew

who worships the Sacred Heart of Christ the blue body of
Krishna the straight back of Ram

the beads of Chango the Nigerian singing Shiva Shiva in a man-
ner which I have invented,

and the King of May is a middleeuropean honor, mine in the
XX century

despite space ships and the Time Machine, because I heard the
voice of Blake in a vision,

and repeat that voice. And I am King of May that sleeps with
teenagers laughing.

And I am the King of May, that I may be expelled from my
Kingdom with Honor, as of old,

To show the difference between Caesar's Kingdom and the
Kingdom of the May of Man –

and I am the King of May, tho' paranoid, for the Kingdom of
May is too beautiful to last for more than a month –

and I am the King of May because I touched my finger to my
forehead saluting

a luminous heavy girl trembling hands who said 'one moment
Mr. Ginsberg'

before a fat young Plainclothesman stepped between our
bodies – I was going to England –

and I am the King of May, returning to see Bunhill Fields and
walk on Hampstead Heath,
and I am the King of May, in a giant jetplane touching Albion's
airfield trembling in fear
as the plane roars to a landing on the gray concrete, shakes &
expels air,
and rolls slowly to a stop under the clouds with part of blue
heaven still visible.
And *tho'* I am the King of May, the Marxists have beat me upon
the street, kept me up all night in Police Station, followed
me thru Springtime Prague, detained me in secret and
deported me from our kingdom by airplane.
Thus I have written this poem on a jet seat in mid Heaven.

May 7, 1965

First Party at Ken Kesey's with Hell's Angels

Cool black night thru the redwoods
cars parked outside in shade
behind the gate, stars dim above
the ravine, a fire burning by the side
porch and a few tired souls hunched over
in black leather jackets. In the huge
wooden house, a yellow chandelier
at 3 A.M. the blast of loudspeakers
hi-fi Rolling Stones Ray Charles Beatles
Jumping Joe Jackson and twenty youths
dancing to the vibration thru the floor,
a little weed in the bathroom, girls in scarlet
tights, one muscular smooth skinned man
sweating dancing for hours, beer cans
bent littering the yard, a hanged man
sculpture dangling from a high creek branch,
children sleeping softly in their bedroom bunks.
And 4 police cars parked outside the painted
gate, red lights revolving in the leaves.

December 1965

Wichita Vortex Sutra

Turn Right Next Corner
>>*The Biggest Little Town in Kansas*
>>>*Macpherson*
Red sun setting flat plains west streaked
>>>with gauzy veils, chimney mist spread
>>>>around christmas-tree-bulbed refineries – aluminum
>>>>white tanks squat beneath
>>>winking signal towers' bright plane-lights,
>>>>>orange gas flares
>>>beneath pillows of smoke, flames in machinery –
>>>>transparent towers at dusk

In advance of the Cold Wave
>>*Snow is spreading eastward to*
>>>>>*the Great Lakes*
>News Broadcast & old clarinets
>>Watertower dome Lighted on the flat plain
>>>car radio speeding acrost railroad tracks –

Kansas! Kansas! Shuddering at last!
>>>>PERSON appearing in Kansas!
>>angry telephone calls to the University
>>Police dumbfounded leaning on
>>>>>their radiocar hoods
>>While Poets chant to Allah in the roadhouse Showboat!
Blue eyed children dance and hold thy Hand O aged Walt
>>who came from Lawrence to Topeka to envision
>>>>Iron interlaced upon the city plain –
>>Telegraph wires strung from city to city O Melville!
>>>>Television brightening thy *rills of Kansas lone*
I come,
>>lone man from the void, riding a bus

hypnotized by red tail lights on the straight
                              space road ahead –
& the Methodist minister with cracked eyes
                        leaning over the table
              quoting Kierkegaard 'death of God'
                        a million dollars
      in the bank   owns all West Wichita
                        come to Nothing!
                  Prajnaparamita Sutra over coffee – Vortex
of telephone radio aircraft assembly frame ammunition
petroleum nightclub Newspaper streets illuminated by Bright
                        EMPTINESS –

Thy sins are forgiven, Wichita!
                Thy lonesomeness annulled, O Kansas dear!
                        as the western Twang prophesied
          thru banjo, when lone cowboy walked the railroad track
                        past an empty station toward the sun
        sinking giant-bulbed orange down the box canyon –
Music strung over his back
          and empty handed singing on this planet earth
                        I'm a lonely Dog, O Mother!
Come, Nebraska, sing & dance with me –
      Come lovers of Lincoln and Omaha,
                        hear my soft voice at last
As Babes need the chemical touch of flesh in pink infancy
    lest they die Idiot returning to Inhuman –
                              Nothing –
So, tender lipt adolescent girl, pale youth,
                        give me back my soft kiss
      Hold me in your innocent arms,
              accept my tears as yours to harvest
              equal in nature to the Wheat
          that made your bodies' muscular bones
                broad shouldered, boy bicept –
          from leaning on cows & drinking Milk
                      in Midwest Solitude –

No more fear of tenderness, much delight in weeping, ecstasy
            in singing, laughter rises that confounds
                        staring Idiot mayors
                                    and stony politicians eyeing
                                    Thy breast,
                                                O Man of America, be born!
Truth breaks through!
            How big is the prick of the President?
                        How big is Cardinal Vietnam?
            How little the prince of the FBI, unmarried all these
            years!
                        How big are all the Public Figures?
                        What kind of flesh hangs, hidden behind their Images?

                                                Approaching Salina,
Prehistoric excavation, *Apache Uprising*
                                    in the drive-in theater
            Shelling Bombing Range   mapped in the distance,
            Crime Prevention Show, sponsor Wrigley's Spearmint
            Dinosaur Sinclair advertisement, glowing green –
South 9th Street lined with poplar & elm branch
                        spread over evening's tiny headlights –
            Salina Highschool's brick darkens Gothic
                        over a night-lit door –
    What wreaths of naked bodies, thighs and faces,
                        small hairy bun'd vaginas,
                        silver cocks, armpits and breasts
                    moistened by tears
                        for 20 years, for 40 years?
Peking Radio surveyed by Luden's Coughdrops
                        Attacks on the Russians & Japanese,
Big Dipper leaning above the Nebraska border,
                        handle down to the blackened plains,
            telephone-pole ghosts crossed
                                    by roadside, dim headlights –
            dark night, & giant T-bone steaks,

and in *The Village Voice*
New Frontier Productions present
Camp Comedy: *Fairies I Have Met.*
Blue highway lamps strung along the horizon east at Hebron
Homestead National Monument near Beatrice –

Language, language
black Earth-circle in the rear window,
no cars for miles along highway
beacon lights on oceanic plain
language, language
over Big Blue River
chanting *La illaha el (lill) Allah hu*
revolving my head to my heart like my mother
chin abreast at Allah
Eyes closed, blackness
vaster than midnight prairies,
Nebraskas of solitary Allah,
Joy, I am I
the lone One singing to myself
God come true –
Thrills of fear.
nearer than the vein in my neck –?
What if I opened my soul to sing to my absolute self
Singing as the car crash chomped thru blood & muscle
tendon skull?
What if I sang, and loosed the chords of fear brow?
What exquisite noise wd
shiver my car companions?
I am the Universe tonite
riding in all my Power riding
chauffeured thru my self by a long haired saint with eyeglasses
What if I sang till Students knew I was free
of Vietnam, trousers, free of my own meat,
free to die in my thoughtful shivering Throne?
freer than Nebraska, freer than America –

May I disappear
in magic Joy-smoke! Pouf! reddish Vapor,
Faustus vanishes weeping & laughing
under stars on Highway 77 between Beatrice & Lincoln –
'Better not to move but let things be' Reverend Preacher?
We've all already disappeared!

Space highway open, entering Lincoln's ear
ground to a stop Tracks Warning
Pioneer Boulevard –
William Jennings Bryan sang
Thou shalt not crucify mankind upon a cross of Gold!
O Baby Doe! Gold's
Department Store hulks o'er 10th Street now
– an unregenerate old fop who didn't want to be a monkey
now's the Highest Perfect Wisdom dust
and Lindsay's cry
survives compassionate in the Highschool Anthology –
a giant dormitory brilliant on the evening plain
drifts with his memories –
There's a nice white door over there
for me O dear!   on Zero Street.

February 15, 1966

II

Face the Nation
Thru Hickman's rolling earth hills
icy winter
gray sky   bare trees lining the road
South to Wichita
you're in the Pepsi Generation   Signum enroute
Aiken Republican on the radio   60,000
Northvietnamese troops now infiltrated but over 250,000
South Vietnamese armed men
our Enemy –

Not Hanoi our enemy
Not China our enemy
The Viet Cong!
McNamara made a 'bad guess'
'Bad Guess?' chorused the Reporters.
Yes, no more than a Bad Guess, in 1962
'8000 American Troops handle the
Situation'
Bad Guess

in 1954, 80% of the
Vietnamese people would've voted for Ho Chi Minh
wrote Ike   years later   *Mandate for Change*
A bad guess in the Pentagon
And the Hawks were guessing all along
Bomb China's 200,000,000
cried Stennis from Mississippi
I guess it was 3 weeks ago
Holmes Alexander in Albuquerque Journal
Provincial newsman
said I guess we better begin to do that Now,
his typewriter clacking in his aged office
on a side street   under Sandia Mountain?
Half the world away from China
Johnson got some bad advice   Republican Aiken sang
to the Newsmen over the radio
The General guessed they'd stop infiltrating the South
if they bombed the North –
So I guess they bombed!
Pale Indochinese boys came thronging thru the jungle
in increased numbers
to the scene of TERROR!
While the triangle-roofed Farmer's Grain Elevator
sat quietly by the side of the road
along the railroad track
American Eagle beating its wings over Asia
million dollar helicopters

a billion dollars worth of Marines
who loved *Aunt Betty*
Drawn from the shores and farms shaking
from the high schools to the landing barge
blowing the air thru their cheeks with fear
in *Life* on Television

Put it this way on the radio
Put it this way in television language
Use the words
language, language:
'A bad guess'

Put it this way in headlines
Omaha World Herald – *Rusk Says Toughness*
Essential For Peace

Put it this way
Lincoln Nebraska morning Star –
Vietnam War Brings Prosperity

Put it *this* way
Declared McNamara   speaking language
Asserted Maxwell Taylor
General, Consultant to White House
Viet Cong losses leveling up three five zero zero per month
Front page testimony February '66
Here in Nebraska same as Kansas same known in Saigon
in Peking, in Moscow, same known
by the youths of Liverpool three five zero zero
the latest quotation in the human meat market –
Father I cannot tell a lie!
A black horse bends its head to the stubble
beside the silver stream winding thru the woods
by an antique red barn on the outskirts of Beatrice –
Quietness, quietness
over this countryside
except for unmistakable signals on radio
followed by the honkytonk tinkle
of a city piano

to calm the nerves of taxpaying housewives of a Sunday
morn.

                        Has anyone looked in the eyes of the dead?
U.S. Army recruiting service sign *Careers With A Future*
        Is anyone living to look for future forgiveness?
Water hoses frozen on the street, the
        Crowd gathered to see a strange happening garage –
        Red flames on Sunday morning
                in a quiet town!
Has anyone looked in the eyes of the wounded?
        Have we seen but paper faces, Life Magazine?
        Are screaming faces made of dots,
            electric dots on Television –
                fuzzy decibels registering
                    the mammal voiced howl
from the outskirts of Saigon to console model picture tubes
        in Beatrice, in Hutchinson, in El Dorado
            in historic Abilene
            O inconsolable!

        Stop, and eat more flesh.
'We will negotiate anywhere anytime'
        said the giant President
        Kansas City Times 2/14/66: 'Word reached U.S. authorities
that Thailand's leaders feared that in Honolulu Johnson might
have tried to persuade South Vietnam's rulers to ease their
stand against negotiating with the Viet Cong.
    American officials said these fears were groundless and
        Humphrey
was telling the Thais so.'
                AP dispatch
                  The last week's paper is Amnesia.

Three five zero zero is numerals
Headline language poetry, nine decades after Democratic Vistas
        and the Prophecy of the Good Gray Poet
            Our nation 'of the fabled damned'
                or else . . .

              Language, language
Ezra Pound the Chinese Written Character for truth
            defined as man standing by his word
                  Word picture: forked creature
                                    Man
          standing by a box, birds flying out
              representing mouth speech
          Ham Steak please waitress, in the warm café.
          Different from a bad guess.
                    The war is language,
                      language abused
                          for Advertisement,
                      language used
                      like magic for power on the planet:
Black Magic language,
              formulas for reality –
                  Communism is a 9 letter word
                          used by inferior magicians with
the wrong alchemical formula for transforming earth into gold
                  – funky warlocks operating on guesswork,
                      handmedown mandrake terminology
                          that never worked in 1956
          for gray-domed Dulles,
                        brooding over at State,
                  that never worked for Ike who knelt to take
                      the magic wafer in his mouth
                          from Dulles' hand
                        inside the church in Washington:
Communion of bum magicians
                    congress of failures from Kansas & Missouri
          working with the wrong equations
          Sorcerer's Apprentices who lost control
                  of the simplest broomstick in the world:
                                    Language
O longhaired magician come home take care of your dumb
      helper

before the radiation deluge floods your livingroom,
                your magic errandboy's
                        just made a bad guess again
            that's lasted a whole decade.

N B C B S U P A P I N S L I F E
        Time Mutual presents
                World's Largest Camp Comedy:
                        Magic In Vietnam —
    reality turned inside out
                changing its sex in the Mass Media
                for 30 days, TV den and bedroom farce
Flashing pictures Senate Foreign Relations Committee room
                Generals faces flashing on and off screen
                                        mouthing language
        State Secretary speaking nothing but language
        McNamara declining to speak public language
                The President talking language,
                    Senators reinterpreting language
                General Taylor *Limited Objectives*
                                Owls from Pennsylvania
                Clark's Face *Open Ended*
                                Dove's *Apocalypse*
                                Morse's hairy ears
        Stennis orating in Mississippi
                    half billion chinamen crowding into the
                                        polling booth,
                Clean shaven Gen. Gavin's image
                                    imagining *Enclaves*
                    Tactical Bombing the magic formula for
                    a silver haired Symington:
        Ancient Chinese apothegm:
                        Old in vain.
                Hawks swooping thru the newspapers
                    talons visible
                wings outspread in the giant updraft of hot air

loosing their dry screech in the skies
over the Capitol
Napalm and black clouds emerging in newsprint
Flesh soft as a Kansas girl's
ripped open by metal explosion –
three five zero zero   on the other side of the planet
caught in barbed wire, fire ball
bullet shock, bayonet electricity
bomb blast terrific in skull & belly, shrapneled throbbing
meat
While this American nation argues war:
conflicting language, language
proliferating in airwaves
filling the farmhouse ear, filling
the City Manager's head in his oaken office
the professor's head in his bed at midnight
the pupil's head at the movies
blond haired, his heart throbbing with desire
for the girlish image bodied on the screen:
or smoking cigarettes
and watching Captain Kangaroo
that fabled damned of nations
prophecy come true –
Though the highway's straight,
dipping downward through low hills,
rising narrow on the far horizon
black cows browse in caked fields
ponds in the hollows lie frozen,
quietness.
Is this the land that started war on China?
This be the soil that thought Cold War for decades?
Are these nervous naked trees & farmhouses
the vortex
of oriental anxiety molecules
that've imagined   American Foreign Policy
and magick'd up paranoia in Peking

and curtains of living blood
surrounding far Saigon?
Are these the towns where the language emerged
from the mouths here
that makes a Hell of riots in Dominica
sustains the aging tyranny of Chiang in silent Taipeh city
Paid for the lost French war in Algeria
overthrew the Guatemalan polis in '54
maintaining United Fruit's banana greed
another thirteen years
for the secret prestige of the Dulles family lawfirm?

Here's Marysville –
a black railroad engine in the children's park,
at rest –
and the Track Crossing
with Cotton Belt flatcars
carrying autos west from Dallas
Delaware & Hudson gondolas filled with power stuff –
a line of boxcars far east as the eye can see
carrying battle goods to cross the Rockies
into the hands of rich longshoremen loading
ships on the Pacific –
Oakland Army Terminal lights
blue illumined all night now –
Crash of couplings and the great American train
moves on carrying its cushioned load of metal
doom
Union Pacific linked together with your Hoosier Line
followed by passive Wabash
rolling behind
all Erie carrying cargo in the rear,
Central Georgia's rust colored truck proclaiming
The Right Way, concluding
the awesome poem writ by the train
across northern Kansas,

                    land which gave right of way
                    to the massing of metal meant for explosion
                              in Indochina —
Passing thru Waterville,
     Electronic machinery in the bus humming prophecy —
            paper signs blowing in cold wind,
                         mid-Sunday afternoon's silence in town
              under frost-gray sky
                             that covers the horizon —
That the rest of earth is unseen,
                          an outer universe invisible,
                  Unknown except thru
                                language
                                   airprint
                                      magic images
        or prophecy of the secret
                    heart the same
                    in Waterville as Saigon one human form:
               When a woman's heart bursts in Waterville
                    a woman screams equal in Hanoi —
On to Wichita to prophesy! O frightful Bard!
          into the heart of the Vortex
               where anxiety rings
                    the University with millionaire pressure,
               lonely crank telephone voices sighing in dread,
          and students waken trembling in their beds
               with dreams of a new truth warm as meat,
               little girls suspecting their elders of murder
                    committed by remote control machinery,
               boys with sexual bellies aroused
                    chilled in the heart by the mailman
     with a letter from an aging white haired General
          Director of selection for service in Deathwar
          all this black language
                         writ by machine!
                    O hopeless Fathers and Teachers

                    in Hué   do you know
                              the same woe too?

I'm an old man now, and a lonesome man in Kansas
          but not afraid
                    to speak my lonesomeness in a car,
               because not only my lonesomeness
                         it's Ours, all over America,
                                   O tender fellows –
                    & spoken lonesomeness is Prophecy
                    in the moon 100 years ago or in
                              the middle of Kansas now.
It's not the vast plains mute our mouths
                         that fill at midnite with ecstatic language
               when our trembling bodies hold each other
                         breast to breast on a mattress –
          Not the empty sky that hides
                              the feeling from our faces
          nor our skirts and trousers that conceal
               the bodylove emanating in a glow of beloved skin,
                    white smooth abdomen down to the hair
                              between our legs,
It's not a God that bore us that forbid
          our Being, like a sunny rose
                    all red with naked joy
          between our eyes & bellies, yes
All we do is for this frightened thing
               we call Love, want and lack –
          fear that we aren't the one whose body could be
                    beloved of all the brides of Kansas City,
                    kissed all over by every boy of Wichita –
     O but how many in their solitude weep aloud like me –
               On the bridge over Republican River
               almost in tears to know
                         how to speak the right language –
          on the frosty broad road

uphill between highway embankments
I search for the language
that is also yours –
almost all our language has been taxed by war.
Radio antennae high tension
wires ranging from Junction City across the plains –
highway cloverleaf sunk in a vast meadow
lanes curving past Abilene
to Denver filled with old
heroes of love –
to Wichita where McClure's mind
burst into animal beauty
drunk, getting laid in a car
in a neon misted street
15 years ago –
to Independence where the old man's still alive
who loosed the bomb that's slaved all human consciousness
and made the body universe a place of fear –
Now, speeding along the empty plain,
no giant demon machine
visible on the horizon
but tiny human trees and wooden houses at the sky's edge
I claim my birthright!
reborn forever as long as Man
in Kansas or other universe – Joy
reborn after the vast sadness of War Gods!
A lone man talking to myself, no house in the brown vastness
to hear,
imaging the throng of Selves
that make this nation one body of Prophecy
languaged by Declaration as Pursuit of
Happiness!
I call all Powers of imagination
to my side in this auto to make Prophecy,
all Lords
of human kingdoms to come

Shambu Bharti Baba naked covered with ash
                    Khaki Baba fat-bellied mad with the dogs
Dehorahava Baba who moans Oh how wounded, How
          wounded
               Sitaram Onkar Das Thakur who commands
                              give up your desire
Satyananda who raises two thumbs in tranquillity
     Kali Pada Guha Roy whose yoga drops before the void
          Shivananda who touches the breast and says OM
Srimata Krishnaji of Brindaban who says take for your guru
     William Blake the invisible father of English visions
     Sri Ramakrishna master of ecstasy eyes
          half closed who only cries for his mother
Chaitanya arms upraised singing & dancing his own praise
          merciful Chango judging our bodies
               Durga-Ma covered with blood
                    destroyer of battlefield illusions
               million-faced Tathagata gone past suffering
     Preserver Harekrishna returning in the age of pain
Sacred Heart my Christ acceptable
               Allah the Compassionate One
                    Jaweh Righteous One
               all Knowledge-Princes of Earth-man, all
     ancient Seraphim of heavenly Desire, Devas, yogis
               & holymen I chant to –
                    Come to my lone presence
                         into this Vortex named Kansas,
I lift my voice aloud,
          make Mantra of American language now,
               I here declare the end of the War!
                    Ancient days' Illusion! –
          and pronounce words beginning my own
               millennium.
Let the States tremble,
     let the Nation weep,
          let Congress legislate its own delight

      let the President execute his own desire –
this Act done by my own voice,
      nameless Mystery –
published to my own senses,
      blissfully received by my own form
    approved with pleasure by my sensations
    manifestation of my very thought
    accomplished in my own imagination
      all realms within my consciousness
      fulfilled
   60 miles from Wichita
      near El Dorado,
       The Golden One,
in chill earthly mist
   houseless brown farmland plains rolling heavenward
       in every direction
one midwinter afternoon Sunday called the day of the Lord –
   Pure Spring Water gathered in one tower
     where Florence is
      set on a hill,
     stop for tea & gas

   Cars passing their messages along country crossroads
    to populaces cement-networked on flatness,
       giant white mist on earth
   and a Wichita Eagle-Beacon headlines
   Kennedy Urges Cong Get Chair in Negotiations
The War is gone,
   Language emerging on the motel news stand,
      the right magic
   Formula, the language known
   in the back of the mind before, now in black print
      daily consciousness
Eagle News Services Saigon –
   Headline Surrounded Vietcong Charge Into Fire Fight
    the suffering not yet ended

                    for others
        The last spasms of the dragon of pain
                shoot thru the muscles
        a crackling around the eyeballs
        of a sensitive yellow boy by a muddy wall
Continued from page one   area
        after the Marines killed 256 Vietcong captured 31
    ten day operation Harvest Moon last December
                        Language language
        U.S. Military Spokesmen
                Language language
                        Cong death toll
        has soared to 100 in First Air Cavalry
        Division's Sector of
                Language language
        Operation White Wing near Bong Son
Some of the
        Language language
                Communist
                        Language language soldiers
charged so desperately
        they were struck with six or seven bullets before they
                fell
Language Language M 60 Machine Guns
                Language language in La Drang Valley
the terrain is rougher infested with leeches and scorpions
                The war was over several hours ago!
Oh at last again the radio opens
        blue Invitations!
                Angelic Dylan singing across the nation
                    'When all your children start to resent you
                    Won't you come see me, Queen Jane?'
        His youthful voice making glad
                        the brown endless meadows
        His tenderness penetrating aether,

soft prayer on the airwaves,
Language language, and sweet music too
even unto thee,
hairy flatness!
even unto thee
despairing Burns!

Future speeding on swift wheels
straight to the heart of Wichita!
Now radio voices cry population hunger world
of unhappy people
waiting for Man to be born
O man in America!
you certainly smell good
the radio says
passing mysterious families of winking towers
grouped round a quonset-hut on a hillock –
feed storage or military fear factory here?
Sensitive City, Ooh! Hamburger & Skelley's Gas
lights feed man and machine,
Kansas Electric Substation aluminum robot
signals thru thin antennae towers
above the empty football field
at Sunday dusk
to a solitary derrick that pumps oil from the unconscious
working night & day
& factory gas-flares edge a huge golf course
where tired businessmen can come and play –
Cloverleaf, Merging Traffic East Wichita turnoff
McConnell Airforce Base
nourishing the city –
Lights rising in the suburbs
Supermarket Texaco brilliance starred
over streetlamp vertebrae on Kellogg,
green jeweled traffic lights
confronting the windshield,

Centertown ganglion entered!
       Crowds of autos moving with their lightshine,
       signbulbs winking in the driver's eyeball –
The human nest collected, neon lit,
            and sunburst signed
     for business as usual, except on the Lord's Day –
Redeemer Lutheran's three crosses lit on the lawn
          reminder of our sins
and Titsworth offers insurance on Hydraulic
by De Voors Guard's Mortuary for outmoded bodies
         of the human vehicle
   which no Titsworth of insurance will customize for
    resale –
So home, traveler, past the newspaper language factory
   under Union Station railroad bridge on Douglas
   to the center of the Vortex, calmly returned
     to Hotel Eaton –
Carry Nation began the war on Vietnam here
          with an angry smashing ax
            attacking Wine –
  Here fifty years ago, by her violence
began a vortex of hatred that defoliated the Mekong Delta –
  Proud Wichita! vain Wichita
    cast the first stone! –
          That murdered my mother
    who died of the communist anticommunist
    psychosis
    in the madhouse one decade long ago
complaining about wires of masscommunication in her head
    and phantom political voices in the air
       besmirching her girlish character.
  Many another has suffered death and madness
    in the Vortex from Hydraulic
       to the end of 17th – enough!

The war is over now —
    Except for the souls
                  held prisoner in Niggertown
still pining for love of your tender white bodies O children of
    Wichita!

February 14, 1966

Uptown

Yellow-lit Budweiser signs over oaken bars,
'I've seen everything' – the bartender handing me change of $10,
I stared at him amiably eyes thru an obvious Adamic beard –
with Montana musicians homeless in Manhattan, teenage
curly hair themselves – we sat at the antique booth & gossiped,
Madame Grady's literary salon a curious value in New York –
'If I had my way I'd cut off your hair and send you to Vietnam' –
'Bless you then' I replied to a hatted thin citizen hurrying to the
        barroom door
upon wet dark Amsterdam Avenue decades later –
'And if I couldn't do that I'd cut your throat' he snarled farewell,
and 'Bless you sir' I added as he went to his fate in the rain,
        dapper Irishman.

                                                        April 1966

Wales Visitation

White fog lifting & falling on mountain-brow
    Trees moving in rivers of wind
                The clouds arise
  as on a wave, gigantic eddy lifting mist
    above teeming ferns exquisitely swayed
                      along a green crag
    glimpsed thru mullioned glass in valley rain –

Bardic, O Self, Visitacione, tell naught
  but what seen by one man in a vale in Albion,
    of the folk, whose physical sciences end in Ecology,
        the wisdom of earthly relations,
    of mouths & eyes interknit ten centuries visible
      orchards of mind language manifest human,
  of the satanic thistle that raises its horned symmetry
  flowering above sister grass-daisies' pink tiny
        bloomlets angelic as lightbulbs –

Remember 160 miles from London's symmetrical thorned tower
    & network of TV pictures flashing bearded your Self
  the lambs on the tree-nooked hillside this day bleating
  heard in Blake's old ear, & the silent thought of Wordsworth
  in eld
                        Stillness
  clouds passing through skeleton arches of Tintern Abbey –
    Bard Nameless as the Vast, babble to Vastness!

All the Valley quivered, one extended motion, wind
          undulating on mossy hills
  a giant wash that sank white fog delicately down red
  runnels
             on the mountainside
  whose leaf-branch tendrils moved asway
        in granitic undertow down –

and lifted the floating Nebulous upward, and lifted the arms
   of the trees
     and lifted the grasses an instant in balance
       and lifted the lambs to hold still
   and lifted the green of the hill, in one solemn wave

A solid mass of Heaven, mist-infused, ebbs thru the vale,
   a wavelet of Immensity, lapping gigantic through
      Llanthony Valley,
the length of all England, valley upon valley under Heaven's
   ocean

                    tonned with cloud-hang,
     – Heaven balanced on a grassblade.
Roar of the mountain wind slow, sigh of the body,
     One Being on the mountainside stirring gently
        Exquisite scales trembling everywhere in balance,
one motion thru the cloudy sky-floor shifting on the million
   feet of daisies,
one Majesty the motion that stirred wet grass quivering
     to the farthest tendril of white fog poured down
        through shivering flowers on the
        mountain's head –

No imperfection in the budded mountain,
     Valleys breathe, heaven and earth move together,
   daisies push inches of yellow air, vegetables tremble,
          grass shimmers green
sheep speckle the mountainside, revolving their jaws with
   empty eyes,
        horses dance in the warm rain,
   tree-lined canals network live farmland,
        blueberries fringe stone walls on
        hawthorn'd hills,
   pheasants croak on meadows haired with fern –

Out, out on the hillside, into the ocean sound, into delicate
   gusts of wet air,

Fall on the ground, O great Wetness, O Mother, No harm on
    your body!
Stare close, no imperfection in the grass,
          each flower Buddha-eye, repeating the story,
            myriad-formed –
Kneel before the foxglove raising green buds, mauve bells
    drooped
      doubled down the stem trembling antennae,
  & look in the eyes of the branded lambs that stare
    breathing stockstill under dripping hawthorn –
I lay down mixing my beard with the wet hair of the
    mountainside,
      smelling the brown vagina-moist ground, harmless,
        tasting the violet thistle-hair, sweetness –
One being so balanced, so vast, that its softest breath
      moves every floweret in the stillness on the valley floor,
    trembles lamb-hair hung gossamer rain-beaded in the grass,
lifts trees on their roots, birds in the great draught
      hiding their strength in the rain, bearing same weight,

Groan thru breast and neck, a great Oh! to earth heart
            Calling our Presence together
    The great secret is no secret
    Senses fit the winds,
        Visible is visible,
    rain-mist curtains wave through the bearded vale,
      gray atoms wet the wind's kabbala
Crosslegged on a rock in dusk rain,
    rubber booted in soft grass, mind moveless,
  breath trembles in white daisies by the roadside,
        Heaven breath and my own symmetric
    Airs wavering thru antlered green fern
drawn in my navel, same breath as breathes thru Capel-Y-Ffn,
      Sounds of Aleph and Aum
        through forests of gristle,
    my skull and Lord Hereford's Knob equal,
        All Albion one.

What did I notice? Particulars! The
        vision of the great One is myriad –
    smoke curls upward from ashtray,
            house fire burned low,
The night, still wet & moody black heaven
                    starless
            upward in motion with wet wind.

July 29, 1967 (LSD) – August 3, 1967 (London)

Elegy for Neal Cassady

OK Neal
    aethereal Spirit
        bright as moving air
         blue as city dawn
happy as light released by the Day
      over the city's new buildings –

Maya's Giant bricks rise rebuilt
             in Lower East Side
    windows shine in milky smog.
        Appearance unnecessary now.

Peter sleeps alone next room, sad.
Are you reincarnate? Can ya hear me talkin?
If anyone had strength to hear the invisible,
And drive thru Maya Wall
    you *had* it –
           What're you now, Spirit?

That were spirit in body –

The body's cremate
         by Railroad track
      San Miguel Allende Desert,
         outside town,
     Spirit become spirit,
         or robot reduced to Ashes.

Tender Spirit, thank you for touching me with tender
    hands
When you were young, in a beautiful body,
      Such a pure touch it was Hope beyond Maya-meat,
      What you are now,
         Impersonal, tender –
you showed me your muscle/warmth/over twenty years ago

when I lay trembling at your breast
                        put your arm around my neck,
– we stood together in a bare room on 103d St.
Listening to a wooden Radio,
                        with our eyes closed
Eternal redness of Shabda
                        lamped in our brains
at Illinois Jacquet's Saxophone Shuddering,
        prophetic Honk of Louis Jordan,
        Honeydrippers, Open The Door Richard
                To Christ's Apocalypse –
The buildings're insubstantial –
That's my New York Vision
                        outside eastern apartment offices
            where telephone rang last night
                    and stranger's friendly Denver Voice
asked me, had I heard the news from the West?

Some gathering Bust, Eugene Oregon or Hollywood
        Impends
                I had premonition.
'No' I said –'been away all week,'
            'you havent heard the News from the West,
                Neal Cassady is dead –'
    Peter's dove-voic'd Oh! on the other line, listening.

Your picture stares cheerful, tearful, strain'd,
                    a candle burns,
                green stick incense by household gods.
Military Tyranny overtakes Universities, your Prophecy
            approaching its kindest sense brings us
                                Down
                to the Great Year's awakening.
Kesey's in Oregon writing novel language
                family farm alone.
Hadja no more to do? Was your work all done?
        Had ya seen your first son?

Why'dja leave us all here?
Has the battle been won?

I'm a phantom skeleton with teeth, skull
        resting on a pillow
            calling your spirit
        god echo consciousness, murmuring
            sadly to myself.

Lament in dawnlight's not needed,
                the world is released,
        desire fulfilled, your history over,
                story told, Karma resolved,
                        prayers completed
        vision manifest, new consciousness fulfilled,
                spirit returned in a circle,
world left standing empty, buses roaring through streets –
        garbage scattered on pavements galore –
Grandeur solidified, phantom-familiar fate
                returned to Auto-dawn,
                    your destiny fallen on RR track
My body breathes easy,
                I lie alone,
                        living
After friendship fades from flesh forms –
heavy happiness hangs in heart,
            I could talk to you forever,
                The pleasure inexhaustible,
                    discourse of spirit to spirit,
                            O Spirit.

Sir spirit, forgive me my sins,
Sir spirit give me your blessing again,
Sir Spirit forgive my phantom body's demands,
Sir Spirit thanks for your kindness past,
Sir Spirit in Heaven, What difference was yr mortal form,
        What further this great show of Space?

Speedy passions generations of
        Question? agonic Texas Nightrides?
        psychedelic bus hejira-jazz,
Green auto poetries, inspired roads?
Sad, Jack in Lowell saw the phantom most —
        lonelier than all, except your noble Self.
Sir Spirit, an' I drift alone:
                Oh deep sigh.

February 10, 1968, 5–5:30 A.M.

Imaginary Universes

Under orders to shoot the spy, I discharged
    my pistol into his mouth.
He fell face down from the position life
    left his body kneeling blindfold.

No, I never did that. Imagined in airport snow,
    Albany plane discharging passengers.

Yes, the Mexican-faced boy, 19
    in Marine cloth, seat next me
Descending Salt Lake, accompanied his
    brother's body from Vietnam.
'The Gook was kneeling in front of me,
    crying & pleading. There were two;
    he had a card we dropped on them.'
The card granted immunity to those
    V.C. surrendering.
'On account of my best friend &
    my brother I killed both Gooks.'
That was true, yes.

February 1969

Rain-wet asphalt heat, garbage curbed cans overflowing

I hauled down lifeless mattresses to sidewalk refuse-piles,
old rugs stept on from Paterson to Lower East Side filled with
     bed-bugs,
gray pillows, couch seats treasured from the street laid back on
     the street
– out, to hear Murder-tale, 3rd Street cyclists attacked tonite –
Bopping along in rain, Chaos fallen over City roofs,
shrouds of chemical vapour drifting over building-tops –
Get the *Times*, Nixon says peace reflected from the Moon,
but I found no boy body to sleep with all night on pavements
     3 A.M. home in sweating drizzle –
Those mattresses soggy lying by full five garbagepails –
Barbara, Maretta, Peter Steven Rosebud slept on these Pillows
     years ago,
forgotten names, also made love to me, I had these mattresses
     four years on my floor –
Gerard, Jimmy many months, even blond Gordon later,
Paul with the beautiful big cock, that teenage boy that lived in
     Pennsylvania,
forgotten numbers, young dream loves and lovers, earthly
     bellies –
many strong youths with eyes closed, come sighing and helping
     me come –
Desires already forgotten, tender persons used and kissed good-
     bye
and all the times I came to myself alone in the dark dreaming
     of Neal Billy Budd
– nameless angels of half-life – heart beating & eyes weeping for
     lovely phantoms –
Back from the Gem Spa, into the hallway, a glance behind
and sudden farewell to the bedbug-ridden mattresses piled
     soggy in day rain.

August 2, 1969

Mugging

Tonite I walked out of my red apartment door on East tenth
    street's dusk –

Walked out of my home ten years, walked out in my honking
    neighborhood

Tonite at seven walked out past garbage cans chained to concrete
    anchors

Walked under black painted fire escapes, giant castiron plate
    covering a hole in ground

– Crossed the street, traffic lite red, thirteen bus roaring by
    liquor store,

past corner pharmacy iron grated, past Coca Cola & Mylai
    posters fading scraped on brick

Past Chinese Laundry wood door'd, & broken cement stoop steps
    For Rent hall painted green & purple Puerto Rican style

Along E. 10th's glass splattered pavement, kid blacks & Spanish
    oiled hair adolescents' crowded house fronts –

Ah, tonite I walked out on my block NY City under humid
    summer sky Halloween,

thinking what happened Timothy Leary joining brain police for
    a season?

thinking what's all this Weathermen, secrecy & selfrighteousness
    beyond reason – F.B.I. plots?

Walked past a taxicab controlling the bottle strewn curb –

past young fellows with their umbrella handles & canes leaning
    against a ravaged Buick

– and as I looked at the crowd of kids on the stoop – a boy
    stepped up, put his arm around my neck

tenderly I thought for a moment, squeezed harder, his umbrella
    handle against my skull,

and his friends took my arm, a young brown companion
    tripped his foot 'gainst my ankle –

as I went down shouting Om Ah Hūṃ to gangs of lovers
　　on the stoop watching
slowly appreciating, why this is a raid, these strangers mean
　　strange business
with what – my pockets, bald head, broken-healed-bone leg, my
　　softshoes, my heart –
Have they knives? Om Ah Hūṃ – Have they sharp metal
　　wood to shove in eye ear ass? Om Ah Hūṃ
& slowly reclined on the pavement, struggling to keep my
　　woolen bag of poetry address calendar & Leary-lawyer
　　notes hung from my shoulder
dragged in my neat orlon shirt over the crossbar of a broken
　　metal door
dragged slowly onto the fire-soiled floor an abandoned store,
　　laundry candy counter 1929 –
now a mess of papers & pillows & plastic car seat covers cracked
　　cockroach-corpsed ground –
my wallet back pocket passed over the iron foot step guard
and fell out, stole by God Muggers' lost fingers, Strange –
Couldn't tell – snakeskin wallet actually plastic, 70 dollars my
　　bank money for a week,
old broken wallet – and dreary plastic contents – Amex card &
　　Manf. Hanover Trust Credit too – business card from
　　Mr. Spears British Home Minister Drug Squad – my
　　draft card – membership ACLU & Naropa Institute
　　Instructor's identification
Om Ah Hūṃ I continued chanting Om Ah Hūṃ
Putting my palm on the neck of an 18 year old boy fingering my
　　back pocket crying 'Where's the money'
'Om Ah Hūṃ there isn't any'
My card Chief Boo-Hoo Neo American Church New Jersey &
　　Lower East Side
Om Ah Hūṃ – what not forgotten crowded wallet – Mobil
　　Credit, Shell? old lovers addresses on cardboard pieces,
　　booksellers calling cards –
– 'Shut up or we'll murder you' – 'Om Ah Hūṃ take it easy'

Lying on the floor shall I shout more loud? – the metal door
    closed on blackness
one boy felt my broken healed ankle, looking for hundred
    dollar bills behind my stocking weren't even there – a
    third boy untied my Seiko Hong Kong watch rough from
    right wrist leaving a clasp-prick skin tiny bruise
'Shut up and we'll get out of here' – and so they left,
as I rose from the cardboard mattress thinking Om Ah
    Hūṃ didn't stop em enough,
the tone of voice too loud – my shoulder bag with 10,000 dollars
    full of poetry left on the broken floor –

November 2, 1974

II

Went out the door dim eyed, bent down & picked up my glasses
    from step edge I placed them while dragged in the store –
    looked out –
Whole street a bombed-out face, building rows' eyes & teeth
    missing
burned apartments half the long block, gutted cellars, hallways'
    charred beams
hanging over trash plaster mounded entrances, couches &
    bedsprings rusty after sunset
Nobody home, but scattered stoopfuls of scared kids frozen in
    black hair
chatted giggling at house doors in black shoes, families
    cooked For Rent some six story houses mid the street's
    wreckage
Nextdoor Bodega, a phone, the police? 'I just got mugged' I said
to the man's face under fluorescent grocery light tin ceiling –
puffy, eyes blank & watery, sickness of beer kidney and language
    tongue
thick lips stunned as my own eyes, poor drunken Uncle minding
    the store!

O hopeless city of idiots empty eyed staring afraid, red beam
      top'd car at street curb arrived –
'Hey maybe my wallet's still on the ground got a flashlight?'
Back into the burnt-doored cave, & the policeman's gray
      flashlight broken no eyebeam –
'My partner all he wants is sit in the car never gets out Hey Joe
      bring your flashlight –'
a tiny throwaway beam, dim as a match in the criminal dark
'No I can't see anything here' . . . 'Fill out this form'
Neighborhood street crowd behind a car 'We didn't see
      nothing'
Stoop young girls, kids laughing 'Listen man last time I messed
      with them see this –'
rolled up his skinny arm shirt, a white knife scar on his brown
      shoulder
'Besides we help you the cops come don't know anybody we all
      get arrested
go to jail I never help no more mind my business everytime'
'Agh!' upstreet think 'Gee I don't know anybody here ten years
      lived half block crost Avenue C
and who knows who?' – passing empty apartments, old lady
      with frayed paper bags
sitting in the tin-boarded doorframe of a dead house.

December 10, 1974

Reading French Poetry

Poems rise in my brain
like Woolworth's 5 & 10¢ Store perfume
O my love with thin breasts
17 year old boy with smooth ass
O my father with white hands
specks on your feet & foul breath bespeak tumor
O myself with my romance
fading but fat bodies remain
in bed with me warm passionless
unless I exercise myself like a dumbbell
O my Fiftieth year approaching
like Tennessee like Andy a failure, big nothing –
very satisfactory subjects for Poetry.

New York, January 12, 1976

'Don't Grow Old'

I

Twenty-eight years before on the living room couch he'd stared
    at me, I said
'I want to see a psychiatrist – I have sexual difficulties –
    homosexuality'
I'd come home from troubled years as a student. This was the
    weekend I would talk with him.
A look startled his face, 'You mean you like to take men's penises
    in your mouth?'
Equally startled, 'No, no,' I lied, 'that isn't what it means.'

Now he lay naked in the bath, hot water draining beneath his
    shanks.
Strong shouldered Peter, once ambulance attendant, raised
    him up
in the tiled room. We toweled him dry, arms under his, bathrobe
    over his shoulder –
he tottered thru the door to his carpeted bedroom
sat on the soft mattress edge, exhausted, and coughed up watery
    phlegm.
We lifted his swollen feet talcum'd white, put them thru pajama
    legs,
tied the cord round his waist, and held the nightshirt sleeve
    open for his hand, slow.
Mouth drawn in, his false teeth in a dish, he turned his head
    round
looking up at Peter to smile ruefully, 'Don't ever grow old.'

II

At my urging, my eldest nephew came
to keep his grandfather company, maybe sleep overnight in the
    apartment.

He had no job, and was homeless anyway.

All afternoon he read the papers and looked at old movies.

Later dusk, television silent, we sat on a soft-pillowed couch,

Louis sat in his easy-chair that swiveled and could lean
back –

'So what kind of job are you looking for?'

'Dishwashing, but someone told me it makes your hands' skin
scaly red.'

'And what about officeboy?' His grandson finished highschool
with marks too poor for college.

'It's unhealthy inside airconditioned buildings under fluorescent
light.'

The dying man looked at him, nodding at the specimen.

He began his advice. 'You might be a taxidriver, but what if a car
crashed into you? They say you can get mugged too.

Or you could get a job as a sailor, but the ship could sink, you
could get drowned.

Maybe you should try a career in the grocery business, but a box
of bananas could slip from the shelf,

you could hurt your head. Or if you were a waiter, you could
slip and fall down with a loaded tray, & have to pay for the
broken glasses.

Maybe you should be a carpenter, but your thumb might get hit
by a hammer.

Or a lifeguard – but the undertow at Belmar beach is dangerous,
and you could catch a cold.

Or a doctor, but sometimes you could cut your hand with a
scalpel that had germs, you could get sick & die.'

Later, in bed after twilight, glasses off, he said to his wife

'Why doesn't he comb his hair? It falls all over his eyes, how can
he see?

Tell him to go home soon, I'm too tired.'

Amherst, October 5, 1978

III

Resigned

A year before visiting a handsome poet and my Tibetan guru,
          Guests after supper on the mountainside
we admired the lights of Boulder spread glittering below
             through a giant glass window –
After coffee, my father bantered wearily
'Is life worth living? Depends on the liver –'
The Lama smiled to his secretary –
It was an old pun I'd heard in childhood.
Then he fell silent, looking at the floor
      and sighed, head bent heavy
           talking to no one –
                'What can you do . . .?'

Buffalo, October 6, 1978

White Shroud

I am summoned from my bed
To the Great City of the Dead
Where I have no house or home
But in dreams may sometime roam
Looking for my ancient room
A feeling in my heart of doom,
Where Grandmother aged lies
In her couch of later days
And my mother saner than I
Laughs and cries She's still alive.

I found myself again in the Great Eastern Metropolis,
wandering under Elevated Transport's iron struts –
many-windowed apartments walled the crowded Bronx
road-way
under old theater roofs, masses of poor women shopping
in black shawls past candy store news stands, children skipped
beside
grandfathers bent tottering on their canes. I'd descended
to this same street from blackened subways Sundays long ago,
tea and lox with my aunt and dentist cousin when I was ten.
The living pacifist David Dellinger walked at my right side,
he'd driven from Vermont to visit Catholic Worker
Tivoli Farm, we rode up North Manhattan in his car,
relieved the U.S. wars were over in the newspaper,
Television's frenzied dance of dots & shadows calmed – Now
older than our shouts and banners, we explored brick avenues
we lived in to find new residences, rent loft offices
or roomy apartments, retire our eyes & ears & thoughts.
Surprised, I passed the open Chamber where my Russian Jewish
Grandmother lay in her bed and sighed eating a little Chicken
soup or borscht, potato latkes, crumbs on her blankets, talking
Yiddish, complaining solitude abandoned in Old Folks House.

I realized I could find a place to sleep in the neighborhood,
    what
relief, the family together again, first time in decades! –
Now vigorous Middle aged I climbed hillside streets in West
    Bronx
looking for my own hot-water furnished flat to settle in,
close to visit my grandmother, read Sunday newspapers
in vast glassy Cafeterias, smoke over pencils & paper,
poetry desk, happy with books father'd left in the attic,
peaceful encyclopedia and a radio in the kitchen.
An old black janitor swept the gutter, street dogs sniffed red
    hydrants,
nurses pushed baby carriages past silent house fronts.
Anxious I be settled with money in my own place before
nightfall, I wandered tenement embankments overlooking
the pillared subway trestles by the bridge crossing Bronx
    River.
How like Paris or Budapest suburbs, far from Centrum
Left Bank junky doorstep tragedy intellectual fights
in restaurant bars, where a spry old lady carried her
Century Universal View camera to record Works
Progress Administration newspaper metropolis
double-decker buses in September sun near Broadway El,
skyscraper roofs upreared ten thousand office windows
    shining
electric-lit above tiny taxis street lamp'd in Mid-town
avenues' late-afternoon darkness the day before Christmas,
Herald Square crowds thronged past traffic lights July noon to
    lunch
Shop under Macy's department store awnings for dry goods
pause with satchels at Frankfurter counters wearing stylish
    straw
hats of the decade, mankind thriving in their solitudes in
    shoes.
But I'd strayed too long amused in the picture cavalcade,
Where was I living? I remembered looking for a house

& eating in apartment kitchens, bookshelf decades ago, Aunt
Rose's illness, an appendix operation, teeth braces,
one afternoon fitting eyeglasses first time, combing wet hair
back on my skull, young awkward looking in the high school
    mirror
photograph. The Dead look for a home, but here I was still
    alive.
    I walked past a niche between buildings with tin canopy
shelter from cold rain warmed by hot exhaust from subway
    gratings,
beneath which engines throbbed with pleasant quiet drone.
A shopping-bag lady lived in the side alley on a mattress,
her wooden bed above the pavement, many blankets and
    sheets,
Pots, pans, and plates beside her, fan, electric stove by the wall.
She looked desolate, white haired, but strong enough to cook
    and stare.
Passersby ignored her buildingside hovel many years,
a few businessmen stopped to speak, or give her bread or yogurt.
Sometimes she disappeared into state hospital back wards,
but now'd returned to her homely alleyway, sharp eyed, old
Cranky hair, half paralyzed, complaining angry as I passed.
I was horrified a little, who'd take care of such a woman,
familiar, half-neglected on her street except she'd weathered
many snows stubborn alone in her motheaten rabbit-fur hat.
She had tooth troubles, teeth too old, ground down like horse
    molars –
she opened her mouth to display her gorge – how can she live
with that, how eat I thought, mushroom-like gray-white
    horseshoe of
incisors she chomped with, hard flat flowers ranged around
    her gums.
Then I recognized she was my mother, Naomi, habiting
this old city-edge corner, older than I knew her before
her life diappeared. What are you doing here? I asked, amazed
she recognized me still, astounded to see her sitting up

on her own, chin raised to greet me mocking 'I'm living alone,
you all abandoned me, I'm a great woman, I came here
by myself, I wanted to live, now I'm too old to take care
of myself, I don't care, what are you doing here?' I
was looking for a house, I thought, she has one, in poor
Bronx, needs someone to help her shop and cook, needs her
        children now,
I'm her younger son, walked past her alleyway by accident,
but here she is survived, sleeping at night awake on that
wooden platform. Has she an extra room? I noticed her cave
adjoined an apartment door, unpainted basement storeroom
facing her shelter in the building side. I could live here,
worst comes to worst, best place I'll find, near my mother in
our mortal life. My years of haunting continental city streets,
apartment dreams, old rooms I used to live in, still paid
        rent for,
key didn't work, locks changed, immigrant families occupied
my familiar hallway lodgings – I'd wandered downhill
        homeless
avenues, money lost, or'd come back to the flat – But couldn't
recognize my house in London, Paris, Bronx, by Columbia
library, downtown 8th Avenue near Chelsea Subway –
Those years unsettled – were over now, here I could live
forever, here have a home, with Naomi, at long last,
at long long last, my search was ended in this pleasant way,
time to care for her before death, long way to go yet,
lots of trouble her cantankerous habits, shameful blankets
near the street, tooth pots, dirty pans, half paralyzed irritable,
she needed my middle aged strength and worldly money
        knowledge,
housekeeping art. I can cook and write books for a living,
she'll not have to beg her medicine food, a new set of teeth
for company, won't yell at the world, I can afford a telephone,
after twenty-five years we could call up Aunt Edie in
        California,
I'll have a place to stay. 'Best of all,' I told Naomi

'Now don't get mad, you realize your old enemy Grandma's
still alive! She lives a couple blocks down hill, I just saw her,
like you!' My breast rejoiced, all my troubles over, she was
content, too old to care or yell her grudge, only complaining
her bad teeth. What long-sought peace!

                                      Then glad of life I woke
in Boulder before dawn, my second story bedroom windows
Bluff Street facing East over town rooftops, I returned
from the Land of the Dead to living Poesy, and wrote
this tale of long lost joy, to have seen my mother again!
And when the ink ran out of my pen, and rosy violet
illumined city treetop skies above the Flatiron Front Range,
I went downstairs to the shady living room, where Peter
    Orlovsky
sat with long hair lit by television glow to watch
the sunrise weather news, I kissed him & filled my pen
    and wept.

October 5, 1983, 6:35 A.M.

Personals Ad

'I will send a picture too
if you will send me one of you'
    — R. CREELEY

Poet professor in autumn years
seeks helpmate companion protector friend
young lover w/empty compassionate soul
exuberant spirit, straightforward handsome
athletic physique & boundless mind, courageous
warrior who may also like women & girls, no problem,
to share bed meditation apartment Lower East Side,
help inspire mankind conquer world anger & guilt,
empowered by Whitman Blake Rimbaud Ma Rainey &
    Vivaldi,
familiar respecting Art's primordial majesty, priapic carefree
playful harmless slave or master, mortally tender passing swift
    time,
photographer, musician, painter, poet, yuppie or scholar —
Find me here in New York alone with the Alone
going to lady psychiatrist who says Make time in your life
for someone you can call darling, honey, who holds you dear
can get excited & lay his head on your heart in peace.

October 8, 1987

Multiple Identity Questionnaire

'Nature empty, everything's pure;
Naturally pure, that's what I am.'

I'm a jew? a nice Jewish boy?
A flaky Buddhist, certainly
Gay in fact pederast? I'm exaggerating?
Not only queer an amateur S&M fan, someone should spank
    me for saying that
Columbia Alumnus class of '48, Beat icon, students say.
White, if jews are 'white race'
American by birth, passport, and residence
Slavic heritage, mama from Vitebsk, father's forebears Grading
    in Kamenetz-Podolska near Lvov.
I'm an intellectual! Anti-intellectual, anti-academic
Distinguished Professor of English Brooklyn College,
Manhattanite, Another middle class liberal,
but lower class second generation immigrant,
Upperclass, I own a condo loft, go to art gallery Buddhist
    Vernissage dinner parties with Niarchos, Rockefellers, and
    Luces
Oh what a sissy, Professor Four-eyes, can't catch a baseball or
    drive a car – courageous Shambhala Graduate Warrior
addressed as 'Maestro' Milano, Venezia, Napoli
Still student, chela, disciple, my guru Gelek Rinpoche,
Senior Citizen, got Septuagenarian discount at Alfalfa's
    Healthfoods New York subway –
Mr. Sentient Being! – Absolutely empty neti neti identity, Maya
    Nobodaddy, relative phantom nonentity

July 5, 1996, Naropa Tent, Boulder, CO

Half Asleep

Moved six months ago left it behind for Peter
He'd been in Almora when we bought it,
an old blanket, brown Himalayan wool
two-foot-wide long strips of light cloth
bound together with wool strings
That after 3 decades began to loosen
Soft familiar with use in Benares & Manhattan
I took it in my hands, searched to match the seams,
    fold them, sew together as I thought
But myself, being ill, too heavy for my arms,
Leave it to housekeeper's repair
    it disappeared suddenly in my hands —
back to the old apartment
where I'd let go half year before

March 7, 1997

Objective Subject

It's true I write about myself
Who else do I know so well?
Where else gather blood red roses & kitchen garbage
What else has my thick heart, hepatitis or hemorrhoids –
Who else lived my seventy years, my old Naomi?
and if by chance I scribe U.S. politics, Wisdom
meditation, theories of art
it's because I read a newspaper loved
teachers skimmed books or visited a museum

March 8, 1997, 12:30 A.M.